Blue Marble

We
have not been thrown out of the garden
but into it to enjoy the beauty of life.
Where else would you find
a blue marble in the
vastness of space growing food
right out of the ground?

NASA/Apollo 17 crew; picture taken by either Harrison Schmitt or Ron Evans -
Full disk view of the Earth taken on December 7, 1972, by the crew of the Apollo 17 spacecraft enroute to the Moon at a distance of about 29,400 kilometers (18,300 mi.) shows Africa, Antarctica, and the Arabian Peninsula.

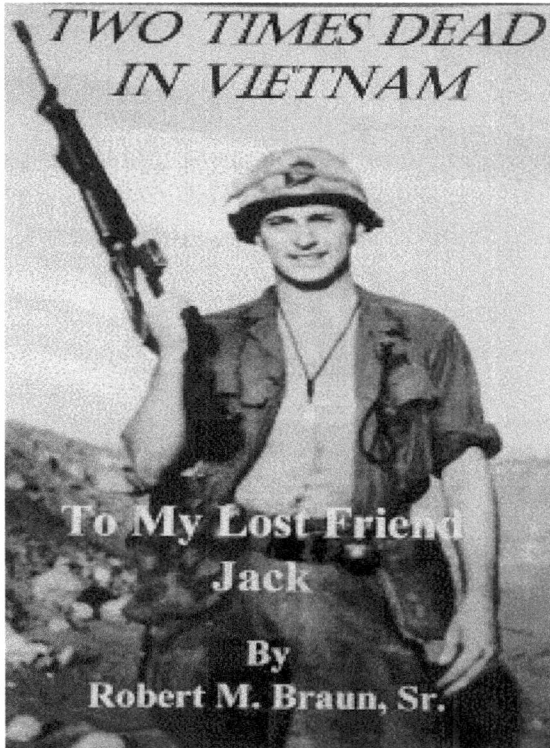

TWO TIMES DEAD
IN VIETNAM

To My Lost Friend
Jack

By
Robert M. Braun, Sr.

By
Robert M. Braun, Sr.

Robert M. Braun, Sr.

ISBN: 978-1-890007-06-5 (sc)
ISBN: 978-1-890007-17-1 (e)
ISBN: 978-1-890007-25-6 (hcbw)
ISBN: 978-1-890007-26-3 (hcc)

Library of Congress Control Number:

Requests for permission to make copies of any part of this work
should be mailed to: Permissions Department, River Magic
Publishing,
P.O. Box #8, Titusville, NJ 08560.
Email: Rivermagic10@gmail.

Edited by
Mary L. Maffei

Mary states: I ensure that every individual that I encounter, is always treated with dignity and respect.

Robert M. Braun, Sr.

To my Children
Kim, Robert, Emily
Grandchildren
Andrew, Jenna

Robert M. Braun, Sr.

Preface   *"Two Times Dead in Vietnam"*

Two Times Dead in Vietnam has been in the making for more than fifty years. Many events have contributed to my writings and the desire to try to send a message; that it is my, and everyone's moral duty/moral responsibility, to help the human race advance into tomorrow. We, as humans, have tried to save other species. Is it not time for us to save the human species, by giving all of us an opportunity to reach our full potential? This desire started when I had to survive two near-death experiences and was given the last rites for both.

The battle to fight for a better world started for me on March 31st, 1970. I have asked many, many times why I was given the gift of life but not my friend Jack Rae Smith. I have concluded that it is to tell the truth while fighting for fairness for all of us who are fortunate enough to be able to enjoy the beauty of our world, and for all those that will follow us.

I first had to fight for my life, then overcome the many injuries I received in Vietnam, on March 31st, 1970, to make it back home, to fight to be considered disabled by the Army while overcoming numerous grand mal seizures, struggle to graduate from college, fight to become a permanent employee of the state of New Jersey, and not leave a man behind.

The battle with the state launched me into writing. After a long frustrating time, I became a permanent New Jersey state employee. I wrote my first published article to help other disabled employees in 1984. Many writings followed that were published. It was the start for me toward finding out why I was given the gift of life that day of March 31st, 1970.

The book *"Two Times Dead in Vietnam"* is divided into seven parts.

The first part is about my battle to become a permanent state employee. It consists of six articles that were in local newspapers along with the piece I wrote entitled, "Equal Employment for the Disabled"; that was published in the Summer 1984 Public Employee Union Newsletter, *Shoptalk.*

The second part of *"Two Times Dead in Vietnam"* is the story of some of my missions, my first and second last rites, going home, and the events that finally led to being recognized as disabled by the Army.

The third part is entitled "Make My Point that War and Violence Are Not the Answer." Included are five of the thirty-seven letters that were published in a newspaper using my Vietnam experiences to prove my point. The five were used to substantiate that both war and violence are not the answer.

The fourth part is devoted to keeping my lost friend and fellow point man's memories alive and not leave a man behind, in the section of the book entitled "Dedicated to Jack Rae Smith."

The fifth part has pictures taken by me, as well as photographs of FSB Pershing, FSB Kien, and "The Bob Hope Christmas Show."

The sixth part includes examples of my other writings from published books: *"Hitting Drills and Much More"*, *"Moral Duty"*, The subtitle of *"Moral Duty"* is, (*"WE are all responsible for our future. WE are all in this together."*), *"Poems Short Stories Art"*, as well as four childrens' books, that were published in February 2024, by River Magic Publishing. They include: *"What is Cool Puppy Doing?"*, *"The Book of Bugs"*, *"Billy Likes the River"*, and *"What is Georgie Doing?"*.

Many of the writings in *"Moral Duty"* deal with the concepts of greed, violence, Machiavellianism, health problems such as Autism and Dementia, what biofeedback is and how I have used it to control my seizure disorder caused by a head injury received in Vietnam, and writings in my fight for fairness for all. The book includes thirty-seven letters that were published in local newspapers and has four chapters: they are "Moral Duty/Moral Responsibility", "Diet and Health", "Power of the Pen", and "The Love of Life".

"Hitting Drills and Much More" is a baseball book/manual that is designed to help educate those who know little about baseball/softball as well as help develop better ballplayers and managers, while teaching the skills to work as a team, and always do your best. It includes stories about three brothers, **forty-five** hitting drills, and the story "With Me Still".

"Poems Short Stories Art", is a collection of thirty-seven poems, short stories, and art that Robert M. Braun, Sr. has created

over the years that expresses his love of life: something he learned while surviving the jungles of Vietnam. His near-death experience inspired him to use the power of the pen to write interesting, informative stories, and articles to help others and tell the truth so that hopefully, we could have a better world. He utilizes the brush to show the beauty of life. His poems are designed to be short, easily understood, and are intended to send a message.

The four children's books, co-authored by myself and Mary L. Maffei, are entitled: *"What is Cool Puppy Doing?"* co-authored by my seven-year-old granddaughter, Jenna M. Braun, *"Billy Likes the River", "The Book of Bugs",* and *"What is Georgie Doing?"* co-authored by my nine-year-old grandson, Andrew M. Braun.

The seventh part is "About the Author", Washington Crossing, New Jersey, my home, and samples of my art.

Six poems are included in the book: "Blue Marble", "How Do We Know?", "More in Life", "Say", "Soldier Boy", and "Life". All were inspired by my love of life: surviving the jungles of Vietnam.

I would like to acknowledge a few new friends who have helped me complete my mission to tell my story and to keep my friend Jack Rae Smith's Scholarship at Wartburg College and memories alive. By obtaining Jack's 1967 High School yearbook I was able to contact some of Jack's childhood friends and family, including Dennis Hoffman, Scott Case, Craig Bergstrom, and Jack's niece, Kimberly Arens.

Others I would like to acknowledge are Scott Leisinger, the Vice President for Institutional Advancement at Wartburg College, the contact for Jack Rae Smith's Scholarship, John Thalacker, a Vietnam Veteran who helped start, and fund the Scholarship, Walter Vincent Brooks, another fellow Vietnam Veteran, and TJ Martin, Dean of Distant Learning at Iowa Central Community College in Fort Dodge, Iowa, who is teaching "Local Vietnam History", and writing a book about Iowa soldiers killed in Vietnam. Also, I want to thank Pastor Warren Curry of The Church of Christ, Clarion, Iowa, who was instrumental in not only finding, but also sending Jack's obituary. It is something I had been searching for over a number of years.

Introduction

As written above, it has been more than fifty years since I served in Vietnam. Over the years I have had three stories about Vietnam published in a national magazine in the late nineties: "The Sun at Last", "Top of the World, Ma!", and "With Me Still". My twin brother Rich, suggested I write about some events that happened while I served there and submit them to a magazine that published stories about Vietnam.

I had just separated from my family and was living in a one-bedroom apartment, so I had plenty of time. That is when I wrote "The Sun at Last", and the other stories followed shortly thereafter. The story was published in the magazine's Christmas issue.

I can still remember receiving a call at work that the story was being published. I was shocked and found it difficult to believe I was able to write a story that was being included in a national magazine.

The first two chapters of *Two Times Dead in Vietnam* are about the start of my tour and are entitled, "Welcome to Vietnam" and "New Day". The characters in these two stories are fictional but based on some events that happened to me. I used fictional characters there because I did not know anyone on the jet that flew me to Vietnam.

The events that occurred in the stories are how I remember them. The remaining stories are about some of the missions and men with whom I served in Vietnam for the four months and eleven days of my tour before I was medevacked out of Vietnam back to the States with shrapnel wounds in my right upper leg, back, groin, head, and a bullet injury in my right bicep.

In a newspaper article in 1983, *Robert Braun Proves You Can Fight City Hall*, the author noted my desire to someday write a book about my experiences. I was given last rites twice in Vietnam.

I was fighting to become a permanent employee for the state of New Jersey and eventually won a permanent position with the state. To help other disabled state employees, I wrote an article that was published in the Summer 1984 Public Employee Union Newsletter, *Shoptalk*.

The article entitled *Equal Employment for the Disabled* launched me into writing. The article is included along with the six articles that were published in local newspapers that had been written about my fight. I was also interviewed after Governor Kean signed a special bill on August 30, 1983 making me a permanent employee of the state of New Jersey. The signing and interview were televised and on national news that evening.

It was more than thirty-nine years ago that the dream of writing a book about my experiences while serving inspired me to use the power of the pen to fight against untruths, injustice, discrimination, and inequalities.

In early 2022, I was able to obtain Jack's 1967 high school yearbook, to find out more about him. This research led me to an article, *Friends Team Up to Revive Fallen Iowa Soldier's Memory*, printed in the Des Moines Register, November 10, 2015. (See "Jack's Memories Live On") The article and yearbook enabled me to contact some of Jack's lifelong friends. This helped me paint a better picture of the person Jack was and why he has left a mark on me and so many others.

Many of the things I found out about Jack were most likely told to me by Jack because we spent so much time together, but my head injury caused many to be wiped out. The more I have found out about Jack, the more memories have come back, filling in some of the parts I do remember of the time we spent together. After finding more history about him, I better understood why we became best friends right away. We had a lot in common, and he was a lot like my twin brother, Rich.

While in Japan recovering from my injuries, **I saw the physical consequences of war**, when I was walking around the Neurology Ward helping other injured soldiers. The loss of Jack – along with the other 58,219 young Americans who did not make it home - also demonstrates the consequences of war, where you had to live life at its most primitive state.

Now, I am fulfilling my dream by writing *"Two Times Dead in Vietnam",* and able to tell the story that affected me, and approximately 2,700,000 other men and women who were ripped from the wombs of home, to fight a senseless war like the one in Vietnam, that almost took my life, and took Jack's.

To help the reader see the country and show what I and all the others that served there experienced, I have included many pictures to my story. Most of the pictures were taken by others; all are from the part of Vietnam that Jack and I patrolled.

Enjoy your reading.

We Fly

We fly to breathe the joys of living.

Around us the garden of earth provides
needs and happiness for life. To enjoy
the smiles, express love always aware the
days are numbered.

So

Why must so much of the wealth belong to
a few? How much nicer things would be
if all could benefit from the riches of
OUR world?

The tiny seed in a universe of darkness.

Table of Contents

How do We Know?

How do we know we are not the seed of life,
whose purpose is to populate the vastness of
high above?

Could it be there are no other voices,
and we are the first in the endless sea of space
to venture beyond our world?

But first we must escape the caves
of savage, violence, greed, and lust.
To grow above our roots of earth to spread our
branches far and wide.

It's just a matter of time before we take the virgin
string of pearls that shines above each night.

Rich   **Me**

More in Life

I saw and came close to death;
it is why I do more in life.

Jack Rae Smith

The First Part
is about my battle to become
a permanent New Jersey
state employee.

Robert M. Braun, Sr.

Headlines in local newspapers:

Fight goes on for Viet Vet, by Jim Goodman, Trenton Times
12/2/1982
Bob Braun's Story, by Ken Carolan, The Trentonian 12/28/1982
NJ Vet Wins Job Battle, by Becky Taylor, Trenton Times,
08/31/1983
Vietnam Veteran Wins Battle for Seniority, by Dave Palombi
Disabled Vietnam Vet Prevails in Civil Service, by Dan Weissman
The Star Ledger 08/31/1983
Robert Braun Proves you can Fight City Hall, by Nancy Freiberg
Princeton Packet 9/16/1983

The following was published in the Summer 1984
Public Employee Union Newsletter *Shoptalk.*

Equal Employment for the Disabled
By Bob Braun

Some members may not be aware of new legislation and regulations that are now available. This legislation would enable them to become permanent state employees without going through normal civil service testing. If you have a physical or psychological handicap that precludes you from taking and/or passing a Civil Service exam, you may now request either a waiver of examination or accommodation.

I know because I am a state employee who has taken advantage of this new legislation and have become permanent with the state by waiver of examination.

My story began in December 1976. I started my employment with the state as a Provisional Auditor III, pending examination, in the Inheritance and Estate Tax section of the Division of Taxation. During the preceding years I applied for and failed numerous Civil Service exams. Due to these failures, I was unable to gain a permanent position with the state, therefore, foregoing seniority, contributions to my pension plan, and other benefits taken for granted by other permanent state employees. I became very

19

frustrated and wanted to give up, wondering if I would ever have a secure position with the state.

A bill was signed by former Governor Brendon T. Byrne, in 1981, which gave the Civil Service Commission the power to waive an exam or provide accommodations for people who demonstrated the capacity to satisfy requirements of the title, yet unable to pass a Civil Service exam due to a physical or psychological handicap.

Since I am a Vietnam Veteran who suffered a head injury during the war, which makes it impossible for me to undergo the prescribed Civil Service testing procedure, the passing of this new legislation gave me new hope.

Following the requirements set forth in the legislation I applied for a waiver of exam, and I received a denial on February 1982 based on what turned out to be an administrative error. I did not get discouraged. I felt that the legislation was implemented for individuals, like myself, who could perform the job but a physical or psychological handicap prevented them from passing a Civil Service test.

I did not agree with the rationale used for the basis for my denial so I wrote a letter to Civil Service requesting a clarification. The response just reiterated the basis used originally.

While this was going on, my superiors informed me that a make-up exam would be made available with certain accommodations. But there was a problem. If I passed the exam and became permanent, I would lose any chance to gain seniority and other benefits. Since I had no other choice, I agreed to take this exam. I passed the exam with the understanding that I would immediately be given a permanent Auditor III title, but this, did not happen.

A hiring freeze was imposed by Governor Kean which prevented me from gaining permanent status with the state. As months went by events seemed to get worse. It began to look like I would not only lose my seniority, pension, and permanent title but also my job and be forced out of my position: all along knowing that my superiors considered me a prototype of the persons for which the legislation was drafted. Finally, due to frustration and depression, I was forced to seek legal advice.

Robert M. Braun, Sr.

I contacted a friend that had recently acquired her law degree and explained my circumstances. She agreed that my treatment was unjust and I was being denied my Due Process. An appeal was filed with the Civil Service Commission along with a request for an oral argument. The oral argument was granted and after a lengthy time period, I was given my waiver of examination. With the waiver I was awarded a permanent appointment of Auditor III, Taxation, effective back to December 1976, a retroactive promotional appointment as Auditor II, Taxation, effective April 1983, and other benefits as if I were permanent when I started my employment with the state.

The granting of my waiver and other benefits that I was entitled to proves that the system does work. But it only works if you stand up for your rights when you have been unjustly treated.

In passing this legislation and setting up regulations the Senate, Assembly, Governor's office, and Civil Service Commission demonstrate that the State of New Jersey is fair to the handicapped and disabled and continues to provide equal employment opportunities, as prescribed by law.

If you feel that a physical or psychological handicap has prevented you from passing a Civil Service exam, I suggest that you stand up, and fight for what is rightfully yours. This legislation was passed for your benefit and is a major step towards achieving equality for the disabled. Remember, the most important factor of this legislation is that a disabled or handicapped person now has the opportunity to gain permanent employment.

Anyone interested in finding out if they are qualified for a waiver of accommodations or if they want to voice support, contact Civil Service of NJ at 44 South Clinton Ave. Trenton, NJ 08625-0310. Their hours are Monday through Friday, 9AM-5PM. Phone number 1-609-292-4144.

> This battle for a permanent position with the state of New Jersey has inspired me to use the **Power of the Pen** to fight against untruths, injustice, discrimination, and inequalities.

Robert M. Braun, Sr.

Fight goes on for Viet Vet

By Jim Goodman
Trenton Times, December 2nd, 1982

"I'm a fighter," says Robert M. Braun. "I have one more fight to win a victory for the rights of a disabled Vietnam Vet."

Braun a 33-year-old Titusville man whose body still carries some of the shrapnel that almost killed him in Vietnam on March 31st, 1970 won the fight for his life that day.

Now he is fighting to keep the job he has held in state government for eight years – a job that is imperiled by the threat of more state layoffs.

The Army gave Braun two Purple Hearts and a Bronze Star for Bravery for his actions in Vietnam. He doesn't march around with those medals but suffers daily from the emotional scars inflicted by the traumatic events which led to earning them.

This condition, described as a "seizure disorder" is attributed to the fact that doctors were unable to safely remove some of the shrapnel lodged near the occipital lobe in his brain.

To CONTROL that condition, Braun must take daily medication. He endured a year of medical treatment in Vietnam, Japan, and the United States, got out of the Army, and earned a degree in business administration at Rider College.

With degree in hand, Braun got a job in the Inheritance and Estate Tax section of the New Jersey Division of Taxation and began a long and still undecided fight for job security.

For eight years, Braun has audited inheritance and estate taxes and his bosses, as several of their memos show, have applauded his efforts "as outstanding".

But those eight years of service to the state may be effectively wiped-out next Tuesday morning by the State Civil Service Commission.

THE COMMISSION is to review Braun's claim that he should be given seniority rights for those eight years even though he only recently passed a Civil Service test that makes him a permanent instead of a temporary employee.

Robert M. Braun, Sr.

Despite his good performance record, Braun was unable to pass a Civil Service test until last October.

"I could do my job but I couldn't take the pressure of the tests," he explains.

When the state, with the help of a new law signed by former Gov. Brendan T. Byrne, allowed the procedures of the tests to be relaxed for disabled veterans with good performance records, Braun passed.

That sounds like a story with a happy ending, but Braun fears it may be just one more frustration.

ACCORDING TO Civil Service rules, his newly acquired Civil Service status is the same as that of any other new employee – not one who has been doing the same job for eight years.

If there are more layoffs in his division, Braun stands to be one of the first to go.

Braun's voice choked and tears filled his eyes as he explained yesterday how difficult it was for him to take the pressure of a test after his Vietnam experience.

"I would go home at night and lay my head down on a pillow and I would see that day in Vietnam again," he remembered. "I would see them dragging away the body of my buddy with his head shot off."

Braun got through Mercer County Community College and graduated from Rider College because his professors let him take tests without any time pressure.

"**I was just** an average student but I did make the Dean's list in my last semester at Rider," he recalls.

Braun earns $21,000 in his job as an auditor with the state, about $4,000 less than if he had been given Civil Service status when he was hired eight years ago.

"It has been frustrating and very hard emotionally on me and my family," he said.

He has a wife, Phyllis, who he began dating when he was a basketball star on the Hopewell Valley High School team and she was a fellow student. They have two children, Kimberly, five, and Robert M. Jr., one.

Robert M. Braun, Sr.

"I would see people hired by the state– people I trained – pass Civil Service, take examinations, and win promotions while I was stuck with the same job.

"IT'S GOOD to see people get ahead," he said. "But hard to take when you can't advance yourself."

Braun's dream of advancement and even a permanent job was hopeless until July, 1981, when the law was enacted to help disabled veterans with psychological problems take tests.

A short time later, Braun applied for permission to take a new Civil Service exam under the provisions of the law.

Approval was granted but the qualifications for his job had been changed. Instead of a college degree and 18 credits in accounting, the new standard was for 21 credits. Braun had 18 credits.

Braun had to fight once again, but this time, he WON!

THE NEW qualifications for the job were waived and Braun after long negotiations with the state officials, was not only allowed to take the test but provided with a calculator and given the exam in private.

He passed with a score of 88.7.

Still there was no happy ending for Braun. He was informed that his "permanent" job title was being held up because of a hiring freeze on state employees.

At that point, Braun appealed to Trenton attorney Jane Kelly for help.

Miss Kelly, who is now carrying Braun's appeal to the Civil Service Commission, was able to get the Civil Service job title approved for Braun.

Bob Braun's Story
By Ken Carolan
The Trentonian, December 28th, 1982

This is a story you don't have to write – it writes itself. And it presents a challenge – to the Legislature, the Governor, and particularly the Civil Service Commission.

Back in 1981 an enlightened Legislature passed an excellent piece of remedial legislation now known as Chapter 204 of the Laws of 1981.

The sponsors of this measure recognized that there were many people in the Civil Service System who perform very well in their jobs but remain only as provisional employees because of their inability to pass a test. In every other way they are completely competent.

REALIZING THE TRUE test of ability is one's level of performance on the actual job, the Legislature authorized the President of the Civil Service Commission to waive the testing requirement when given an employee's performance record and evaluations by his or her supervisors attesting to their capability.

The employees must also submit suitable medical proof concerning their disability which hinders or prevents them from passing the required tests for permanent status and promotions.

If they remain "Provisionals"- and many do for many years – they never receive benefits such as the state contribution to their pension, insurance, and of course, promotions and salary increments. They are also the first to be discharged when a reduction in force is implemented.

They may be rated "outstanding" by their superiors but obviously their job security is far less outstanding.

This is the situation that Bob Braun has faced for the past eight years. He was hired as an Auditor III for the Department of Taxation in 1976 on a provisional basis. He is still an Auditor III – he is still on a provisional basis.

He has seen people he trained promoted above him and enjoy large salary increases as well as all the benefits he does not receive. Those people could pass the Civil Service tests. Bob Braun couldn't.

On March 31st, 1970 he was hit by shrapnel while in combat in Vietnam. He was severely wounded in the head and back. One piece of shrapnel entered the occipital lobe of his brain. The doctors said it could not be removed without endangering Bob's life. He still carries that souvenir of the war, in his head, during which he received two Purple Hearts and a Bronze Star for Bravery.

SEVERAL DOCTORS HAVE CERTIFIED that as a result of pressure from that piece of shrapnel, Bob suffers from a seizure disorder. Fortunately, it is successfully controlled by medication but the doctors have stated that because of this disorder, his ability to take formal written examinations has been permanently and irreparably impaired.

Bob felt certain that when the remedial legislation mentioned above was passed by the Legislature he would surely qualify for the waiver to permanent status. So far it hasn't happened despite his long performance record and a file full of very favorable evaluations, including his latest "outstanding".

However, he is looking forward to the New Year with a little more optimism.

RECENTLY HIS ATTORNEY, Jane Kelly, of the firm Sterns, Herbert, and Weinroth, made an eloquent appeal before the Civil Service Commission. She presented hearing officers with a letter from one of Bob's superiors describing him as "a prototype of the person for whom this remedial legislation was drafted."

And the young lawyer reminded the Commission, of Governor Kean's recent commitment to helping Vietnam Veterans, when on November 4th, he paid tribute to them and pledged, "That the state of New Jersey desires to focus awareness on its Vietnam Veterans who endured hardships and made sacrifices on behalf of the principles of freedom and self-determination."

That is where the story of Bob Braun stands today. Certainly, the remedial legislation was sorely needed and will assist many loyal Civil Service employees.

And certainly, the Governor's concern for Vietnam Veterans is very commendable.

BUT NEITHER THE legislation nor the Governor's words mean a damn thing unless both are fully implemented.

Jane Kelly made her plea on behalf of Bob Braun, all handicapped persons in state employment, and especially our Vietnam Veterans.

So far, all those people have received from the state is rhetoric. What they obviously need are results.

Robert M. Braun, Sr.

NJ Vet Wins Job Battle

By Becky Taylor
State House Reporter, Trenton Times
August 31st, 1983

Governor Thomas H. Kean yesterday untangled the red tape which has kept Vietnam Veteran Robert M. Braun of Titusville in a job limbo for the last seven years.

Braun, who earned two Purple Hearts and a Bronze Star for Bravery in action in Vietnam, hasn't been able to win permanent status as a state employee since he took a job as an auditor in the State Taxation Division in 1976.

Yesterday Braun's employment problems ended when Governor Kean signed a bill granting him permanent status, a promotion, and a retroactive raise.

"Mr. Braun has been caught up in a truly unique situation," Kean said. "I am delighted to be able, with the stroke of a pen, to slice through the kind of red tape which has kept Mr. Braun from attaining what is rightfully and properly his."

As a result of the bill sponsored by Senator Walter E. Foran, R-Hunterdon, and Senator Barbara Kalik, D-Burlington, Braun will be promoted from the "Auditor III" to "Auditor II" position. His salary will jump from about $22,000 to $24,000 annually.

After the ceremony, Braun described himself as - "very relieved."

"For the past seven years," he said, "he felt he was being more or less punished for being in Vietnam."

While serving in Vietnam, he was wounded in the head and back. A piece of shrapnel which was lodged in his brain, remains there to this day, since it cannot be safely removed.

The resulting disorder "has permanently impaired Mr. Braun's ability to take formal written examinations," according to a memo from the Governor's Council Office. "However, Mr. Braun was able to graduate from Rider College because his professors allowed him extra time to take tests."

In 1976, Braun took a job as state auditor on a provisional basis. Because he couldn't finish a written civil service examination

Robert M. Braun, Sr.

within the allowed time frame, he wasn't able to gain permanent job status.

But his job performance didn't suffer as a result of his war-related injuries. He consistently won satisfactory to outstanding ratings in job performance evaluations.

In the meantime, other Civil Service and hiring quirks compounded Braun's employment problems. Over the years, Braun saw many employees with less experience, some of whom he trained, win promotions for which he wasn't entitled, because he could not pass the tests.

The bill signed yesterday makes up for lost time. It provides about $8,000 in retroactive pay, according to Carl Golden, the Governor's press secretary. And, it gives Braun the permanent status he has sought since 1976.

"My apologies this wasn't done seven years ago," Governor Kean said during yesterday's ceremony. "Mr. Braun has served his country in the military and we owe him a debt of gratitude for that service," Kean said. "He is now serving the people of the state as their employee, and the very least we can do is assure he will be able to continue that service."

Vietnam Veteran Wins
Battle for Seniority
Trenton Times, by Dave Palombi, August 31, 1983

For Robert M. Braun, a decorated Vietnam Veteran and self-described "fighter", the long battle for a fair shake is finally over.

Governor Thomas H. Kean yesterday signed legislation paving the way for state employee Braun, 34, of Titusville, to gain a promotion and receive retroactive salary payments which he had been denied because injuries he suffered in Vietnam had impaired his ability to take a written Civil Service test.

Braun, who holds two Purple Hearts and a Bronze Star for Bravery, still suffers from a "seizure disorder" which he attributes to the fact that doctors were unable to remove shrapnel lodged in his brain.

"Mr. Braun has been caught up in a truly unique situation," Kean said at a news conference yesterday. "I am delighted to be able with the stroke of a pen, to slice through the kind of red tape which had kept Mr. Braun from attaining what is rightfully and properly his."

BRAUN, an auditor with the State Division of Taxation for nine years, will be promoted to the rank of Auditor II with a salary of $24,000. He formerly was Auditor III with a salary of $22,000.

Braun, married and the father of two children, was injured in Vietnam on March 31st, 1970. He endured a year of medical treatment in Vietnam, Japan, and the United States before leaving the Army and earning a degree in business administration at Rider College.

Braun then got his job with the Division of Taxation, where his work has been called "outstanding," according to memos filed by his bosses.

After auditing inheritance taxes for eight years, Braun finally passed a written Civil Service test, after a law was passed relaxing the procedures for disabled Veterans with good performance records.

"I could do my job but I couldn't take the pressure of the tests," Braun said.

After this success, however, Braun began the fight for seniority rights for the eight years he had worked prior to passing the test – a fight which was won yesterday.

Kean's decision gives Braun permanent status and qualifies him for state benefits such as health insurance and pension.

Robert M. Braun, Sr.

Disabled Vietnam Vet
Prevails in Civil Service

By Dan Weissman

The Star Ledger , August 31st, 1983

Robert M. Braun of Titusville, NJ received two Purple Hearts and a Bronze Star in Vietnam and came home from the war with shrapnel lodged in his brain from a March 31st, 1970 wound that almost killed him.

Yesterday the Vietnam Veteran received special consideration under a bill signed by Governor Thomas Kean that will allow him to become a permanent tax division auditor, and to receive the promotions, and raises his war-related disorder had prevented him from earning.

Braun's case was described by Kean as "truly unique" because of his inability to meet conditions of the Civil Service regulations. He was able to graduate from Rider College, NJ with a degree in business administration because his professors gave him extra time to take tests.

The war injuries left him impaired to the extent he cannot complete a formal written examination in the time allotted. According to a memo drafted by the Governor's office, the "piece of shrapnel, which cannot be safely removed, has caused a condition described as a seizure disorder which is controlled by daily medication."

The 33-year-old Braun, who has been auditing inheritance taxes since 1976 as a provisional employee, had little to say after Kean signed the bill which "cut through the red tape" that locked him into a nonpermanent job category.

His only comments were "I would like to thank the Governor. I have gone through a lot of problems; I think this will solve them."

Throughout the years, Braun has encountered a series of setbacks. First, he was ineligible to take the auditor's exam because the requirements for permanent status called for an increase of accounting credits from 18 to 21.

30

That change was introduced after a law was signed that allowed the Civil Service Commission to waive an examination for persons who demonstrated their ability to do a job but could not take the test for some specific physical or psychological reason. The memorandum, prepared by assistant counsel Susan Matalucci, offered further insight into Braun's frustrations.

"Mr. Braun's request for a waiver was denied on the basis that he did not have the requisite number of accounting credits," the memo said. "However, Mr. Braun was subsequently permitted to take a make-up examination under special circumstances, which he successfully passed. Due to a hiring freeze, however, Mr. Braun has not yet received permanent Civil Service classification."

Governor Kean, who signed the bill at a public ceremony in his outer office, said he was "delighted to be able, with the stroke of a pen, to slice through the kind of red tape which has kept Mr. Braun from attaining what is rightfully and properly his."

"With the signing of this bill, Mr. Braun will receive permanent status and qualify for the same benefits as all other state employees."

The Governor added, "Mr. Braun has served his country in the military and we owe him a debt of gratitude for that service. He is now serving the people of the state as their employee and the very least we can do is assure he will be able to continue that service."

Robert Braun of Titusville, right, talks with Maj. Gen. Francis Gerard, head of the New Jersey Department of Defense, before the ceremony when Gov. Kean signed a bill allowing Braun to be promoted.

Robert M. Braun, Sr.

Robert Braun Proves You Can Fight City Hall
By Nancy Freiberg
Princeton Packet, September 16th,1983

In Vietnam, Robert Braun was a fighter. In addition to the two Purple Hearts and a Bronze Star he earned for Bravery in that war, he carried home with him a permanent reminder – a piece of shrapnel lodged in his brain.

When he returned to the United States, he expected the battle to be over. Instead, he found it had just begun.

The shrapnel in his brain caused a seizure disorder, controlled by medication, but making it impossible for him to concentrate for long periods of time.

By having professors give him extra time to take tests, Mr. Braun was able to get a degree in Business Administration from Rider College, New Jersey, and shortly afterward was given a temporary position as an Auditor III in the state Division of Taxation dealing with inheritance tax.

But he soon found himself surrounded by people he had trained who were being promoted, while he remained in the same position. His enemy became not the Viet Cong with a gun, but a document: the Civil Service test required for each promotion, **MR. BRAUN,** who lives in Titusville, NJ with his wife and two children, had already taken and failed the test several times. "It was very frustrating," said the 34-year-old Mr. Braun, "Every lunch, every break, I studied and I kept failing the test."

"I became very discouraged," he added. "I felt that I was being punished for Vietnam."

The disorder made it impossible for Mr. Braun to pass the test in the allotted time.

In 1981 former Governor Brendan T. Byrne signed a bill that seemed to be the answer to Mr. Braun's prayers. The bill allowed the Civil Service Commission to waive examinations for people who demonstrated their capacity to function in position, but who are unable, for psychological or physical reasons, to pass a Civil Service test.

So, after learning about the bill Mr. Braun applied for a waiver of examination in December of 1981. Two months later, the

32

request was denied. During the time he was fighting for his promotion, and taking and failing the test, the 18 credits in accounting required for the job had been changed to 21.

AFTER COMMUNICATING back and forth with Civil Service officials, Mr. Braun was informed he could take a "make-up" test under which only 18 accounting credits were required. He was also told if he refused to take the test, he would lose his job.

In March of 1982 he took the examination without time constraints and passed with a score of 88.7. It took until May for him to get official notice of the score.

"After I passed the special test, I was told I'd be promoted quickly," Mr. Braun said. But in July, the Governor imposed a hiring freeze, further delaying his promotion.

"One event led to another," Mr. Braun said.

It wasn't until Governor Thomas H. Kean signed a special bill on August 30th, 1983 that he received his promotion to Auditor II, along with back pay.

"I'M EXTREMELY HAPPY I got a response and things worked out," Mr. Braun said. "I was an individual caught up in the system."

Although the "system" has been changed in New Jersey and he received his promotion, Mr. Braun is ready to fight again. "Now that it's (the bill) been implemented in New Jersey, there's no reason why others can't benefit," he said.

Mr. Braun has contacted Rep. Chris Smith about the possibility of introducing a similar bill in Congress. "I don't want to do it myself," he said. "I'm trying to get other people involved."

Mr. Braun has also contacted the commander of the Disabled American Veterans in reference to such a bill. He said the New Jersey law has already allowed 15 people to be promoted through special arrangements with the Civil Service.

MICHAEL ARCIERI, Vice Principal of Hopewell Valley Central High School, was one of the people Mr. Braun turned to for help. "I had Robert as a student in the 1960s and he came to me for counsel, Mr. Arcieri said. "I encouraged him because I thought he was right."

"Bob was always known as being a tough, but clean competitor," he said. Mr. Arcieri encouraged Mr. Braun to contact his personal friend, former state Sen. Joseph P. Merlino, who in turn helped the Veteran cut through the red tape.

Mr. Braun also said his supervisor, Archie J. Brackel and William R. Mulholland, superintendent of the Inheritance Tax Division were behind him "100 percent."

Mr. Braun said he "ignores" people that think the New Jersey law will result in employees being hired who are incompetent. "I can understand people feeling that way," he said, "They just don't know. That's why I want to have people educated."

HE EXPLAINED that before an applicant can be considered for waiver of examination, statements from a doctor indicating why the applicant cannot undergo the testing procedure, and appointment authority concerning the applicant's competency for the position, are required.

The applicant must also agree to undergo any additional physical and/or psychological examinations deemed necessary by the President of the Civil Service.

Mr. Braun said he hopes someday to write a book about his experiences. "I was given last rites twice in Vietnam," he explained.

When Governor Thomas H. Kean signed the bill that gave Mr. Braun his promotion, he said, "Mr. Braun has served his country in the military and we owe him a debt of gratitude for that service. He is now serving the people of the state as their employee and the very least we can do is assure he will be able to continue that service."

The Governor's signature ended a long and frustrating ordeal for a man willing to fight for what he believed he deserved. For Mr. Braun, it was a battle well fought and won.

Vietnam Veteran Robert Braun has had an uphill fight to further his career, but he has won.

Soldier Boy

Waste, waste, young soldier boy
never return the same,
nightmares of human carrion
like maggots eating flesh of Boys
ripped from wombs of home.
Heroes lined in black plastic bags,
numbers for each night.
Protest at Kent State, Washington DC
Advance the cause of truth.
Let the souls beyond the graves protect
our future youth.

This poem is dedicated to **Jack Rae Smith**
and all those that made the ultimate
sacrifice for our country and democracy.

The first two chapters, *Welcome to Vietnam* and *New Day* are with fictional characters that are based on true events. The following stories are about my tour.

I am calling the book about my tour in Vietnam **"Two Times Dead in Vietnam"** because, I was given my last rites twice while serving there. The first was when I was returned from the field to Cu Chi, the Twenty-Fifth's Division Headquarters to the 12th Evacuation Hospital with a head injury and other wounds on March 31st, 1970.

The second time was when I was being sent to a hospital in Japan and had a grand mal seizure. I was VIP, via Medevac Helicopter, back to the hospital in Vietnam.

One of my best friends, who had worked as the Vice-President of a publishing company in Philadelphia, suggested that I should call the book *Two Times Dead*. I lost my good friend, Bill Stinson a number of years ago but, have him live on, by naming the title of this book, *"Two Times Dead in Vietnam"*.

The Second Part

is the story of some of my missions, my first and second last rites, going home, and events that finally led to being recognized as disabled, by the Army.

Robert M. Braun, Sr.

TWO TIMES DEAD
In VIETNAM

Private Robert M. Braun, Sr.
in Basic Training

WELCOME TO VIETNAM

"**F**asten your seat belts. The present temperature is 87 degrees and the time is 0134 hours. Below, if you look out the windows to the left, you'll see Saigon, the capital. After the plane has landed and comes to a stop, please remain seated. You'll receive instructions how to proceed. Welcome to Vietnam," announced the captain.

"What the hell does that mean? Remain seated until receiving instructions?" asked Bill, a short thin nineteen-year-old from Indian Lake, New York, who wore thick wire rimmed glasses and was sitting in the aisle seat.

Jim, a slightly overweight twenty-year-old from Cleveland, Ohio, with acne scarred face and large bulging eyes who sat in the middle seat answered, "The hell if I know."

Not wanting to talk to anyone, Bob glared out the window at the lights below. He took a long drag off his cigarette and then blew out the light blue smoke that added to the heavy cloud of smoke that filled the plane, then crushed out the unknown number of a chain of cigarettes that filled the ashtray. He turned toward the window to the outside world and the mixed emotions he found himself feeling.

If the captain hadn't announced that it was Vietnam below you would have never known. There were thousands maybe millions of specks of lights that stretched as far as the eye could see. Bob knew that a war was going on down there so he strained to see some kind of explosion or fire, something that looked different than flying over Chicago or New York. It looked the same.

The four engines of the jet began to whine and the plane began its descent. Bob knew that in a very short time he would be in a country thousands of miles from his home, alone, wondering if he would survive the year.

He was an inexperienced twenty-year-old small town Jersey boy drafted into the Army like thousands of other young Americans during the late 60's and early 70's: part of the forty-five thousand reinforcements that General Harold K. Johnson, Army Chief of Staff, said would be needed to convince Hanoi that it was not worth the price to continue fighting. Ref. 1

Bob had been only a year out of high school, never away from his family, six months into the Army, flying for only the third time, alone, into a country torn apart by civil war. Fate, events totally out of his control, had brought him to this Asian hellhole. Now, he must rely on instinct, his natural aptitude to respond in ways that are necessary for his survival, and an animating force that had been passed to him through thousands of years.

The completely filled jet slowed and bounced as it banked left. Below you could see the dark black line of the Saigon River snaking through the white specks of lights. As the plane descended, the lights became larger and the cars and trucks moving on the roads below became visible.

In a very short time, the plane would be landing. Soon, Bob would be fighting and risking his life for his country, protecting the ability to move or choose without outside interference, fighting for his family and protecting their freedom, helping to stop the growth of Communism, defeating Hanoi and Ho Chi Minh, to do what thousands of other young men and women had tried but failed to do before him.

Bob's thoughts drifted back to a sunny afternoon in late August 1969. He had just spent a satisfying weekend with his girlfriend and seeing his family. She was returning him to basic training at Fort Dix, New Jersey, from a weekend pass. They were sitting in the parking lot in her light blue Volkswagen Beetle. She was trying to talk him into deserting, and running away with her to Canada.

"Come on Bob, don't you want to go? We could leave right now and be in Canada by tomorrow. I have some money in the bank and I'm sure my father would help us. Once there we could get married and live in Canada until the war is over. I've heard a lot about other guys that have left with their wives or girlfriends to stay out of Vietnam. You know I can't stand the idea of you being so far away and maybe even going to Vietnam and getting killed," she pleaded as tears filled her light blue eyes.

Alice and Bob were from different worlds. He was from a large family. During most of his childhood he had little and spent most of his time playing and exploring the woods and fields around his home. He earned money trapping animals and mowing lawns.

While working at the New Jersey Washington Crossing State Park, during the summers of high school, he learned that America had its roots in the area he called home: that our country's forefathers had suffered tremendous hardships fighting for the freedoms many now take for granted. He respected our founding fathers for their sacrifices to fight for what they believed. It was only natural for him to continue the fight to protect the American way.

Alice, on the other hand, was from an affluent family and being the baby in her family she was accustomed to getting her own way. She attended a small private girls' school and was more comfortable with the better things in life, like going on shopping trips to New York City, and to the shows on Broadway.

Her father was the president and owner of a small manufacturing company that manufactured plastic and rubber hoses. Her mother was against the war and participated in the October 21st, protest march in Washington, D.C. Both of her older brothers did not get drafted because of college deferments and their father's connections. Ref. 2

They had been dating each other for a little over a year and their relationship had become a little too serious. She loved him because of his burning desire to better himself and how he treated her as an equal, always encouraging, and helping her to reach her goals. He was the first man to respect her as a person and was not afraid to stand up to her.

Bob had no intention of settling down, let alone running away with her and never seeing his family. So, he slowly turned and looked directly into her tearing blue eyes. "I'm sorry but I can't go. If I run to Canada with you how would I ever be able to see my family or set foot in this country again?

Last November they sentenced a guy to two and a half years of hard labor for just refusing to go to Vietnam. He didn't even desert and he was given that long. Plus, it is my duty. What would my family think of me and how long would I be able to live with myself, if I deserted and went to Canada with you? I know it sounds corny but, I have been asked to serve my country and protect its freedom."

"Oh, bullshit," screamed Alice, "You have already been brainwashed into believing it's alright to fight and kill and, I really don't care about your family. I just know you're going to Vietnam and I'm totally against that goddamn war. How am I supposed to survive without you, knowing you are there? If you don't go to Canada with me tonight, I can't promise that I will wait for you."

"I have not been brainwashed into believing it's right to kill and if that's the way you want it, I'm sorry, but I can't and won't go," answered Bob. "I guess it's better we cool it then, I don't want to be attached to anyone anyway."

Alice began to cry; sorry she ever brought it up. Bob put his arms around her and stroked her long blonde hair. He knew he was going to Vietnam and couldn't go to Canada with her. He felt it was better to go it alone.

One night after a high school basketball game, while he was in his senior year of high school, he had a dream, a nightmare. He saw himself in a firefight in Vietnam. He remembered the fighting, the rat-ta-tat of machine guns, the sound of bombs, the smell of sulfur, and a flash of a large explosion, how he suddenly awakened to find himself sitting up in his bed dripping wet with sweat. Bob never told anyone about this dream.

Later that afternoon, he got his orders. He was ordered to report to Fort Lewis, Washington for Advanced Infantry Training, a sure sign that he would be going to Vietnam.

Bob saw Alice a few more times but it was never the same. By the time he finished his Advanced Infantry Training, he was alone to face whatever lie ahead.

Jim, the guy next to Bob said, "Goddamn, I'm scared. I'm so scared that I'm almost ready to shit my pants. If I knew it was going to be like this I would've listened to my father and gone to college like he wanted. I can't believe I have to spend a whole year in this godforsaken place. At least I am not infantry like you Bob. How in the hell can you be so calm?"

Bob was afraid, but he was also excited. His blood rushed through his veins and he felt a sense of adventure. He had trained hard for this knowing for some time that he would be drafted into the Army and that he would fight in Vietnam. All of his life he had made his body hard, playing baseball, basketball, football and competing with his brothers: spending hours and days in the fields and woods around his home and learning many things that would help him to survive the jungles.

He was a soldier, a fighting machine. It's no wonder he had earned outstanding trainee of his basic training cycle, bettering over three-thousand other trainees by receiving the highest combined physical and academic scores: recording expert in all firearms tests, gaining knowledge and skills in hand-to-hand combat and other fighting tactics so fast, he helped to train his fellow trainees. He was primed, ready to go, as if it was always in his blood to be a fighter, a warrior.

The lights now flashed by as the plane approached the runway. Everyone was quiet. No one knew what to expect. No one knew if they would ever see home and their family again: whether they would become a number in the body count of Americans shown on TV each night.

Bob watched with crossed fingers as the plane approached the runway then felt it jerk as the wheels touched down, and heard the engines roar as they were thrust into reverse to slow the aircraft down. He was in a country thousands of miles from home, a place that had taken the lives of thousands of young Americans, yet was not declared a war.

The plane taxied off the runway. Outside Bob could see fighter jets, propeller-driven dive bombers, small artillery spotters, and large planes carrying enormous radar domes on their backs, types of aircraft that were new to Bob. There was a lot of activity as ground crews unloaded huge transport planes sitting with their rear loading ramps opened wide. The men unloading the C-150 transport planes paid little attention to the jet as it rolled by, intent in only unloading the cargo.

The C-150 transport planes were huge, painted camouflage green, their wings sagging because they were so long. Bob wondered how they could fly because they were so immense. They were the lifeline of the men bringing in food, clothing, weapons, and many other things necessary for the survival of the five-hundred thousand men now stationed and fighting in Vietnam.

Robert M. Braun, Sr.

Bob felt a sense of heat, since his blood burnt its way throughout his veins. He was there to fight. Being infantry, he knew he would fight in the jungles and rice paddies. He spent many nights watching the fighting in the jungles and cities of Vietnam and watched the battles during the 68 Tet Offensive, on TV. He also watched the protests of the war that was covered on the news each night and the body count of young American soldiers continually increased.

He felt a mixture of excitement, fear, desperation, hopelessness, but most of all he felt alone, torn from his family and friends: forced to fight in a conflict he knew little about, or understood. He couldn't turn back; he had to move forwardly to face whatever lie ahead.

Jim, the guy next to Bob said, "Boy am I glad I won't be fighting in the jungles. It's bad enough I've got to be here let alone going into the jungles and possibly being shot. Look at that chopper, that one with the holes in its windshield, looks like it got too close to the action."

Bill, the guy in the aisle seat said, "I'm with you man. Being a cook, I won't have to worry about eating or being shot at. I may even gain some weight here."

Bob, not taking his eyes off the sights outside said, "You guys may be right, but I was told by a spec-six during basic training that a lot of guys stationed in the rear, like you two, never make it back home. Charlie sneaks in at night and cuts the throats of sleeping pencil pushers.

Do you know the Vietcong are getting rockets from Russia, some with a range of nine miles? So, don't relax too much while you are here." No one laughed since they knew it was true.

Bill said, "At least we'll have a roof over our heads and maybe even hot running water. Not like you, all you'll have is a M-16 and Charlie behind every bush shooting at you."

The jet came to a stop. Outside Bob saw a large group of men dressed in Army dress uniforms. Bob said, "What the hell are those guys doing standing out here in the middle of the night in dress uniforms?"

Bob found out later the men he saw were men who had completed their tour and were returning to the states on the plane that brought their replacements. Looking over the loose formation Bob saw very few wearing the blue braid shoulder ribbon of the Army infantry.

Suddenly, a loud voice of a sergeant wearing jungle fatigues startled Bob from his thoughts. "Welcome to Tan Son Nhut Air Force Base and South Vietnam. All of you men are to file out of the plane, line up outside, and wait for buses to take you to barracks for the night. Tomorrow you'll be shipped to replacement centers and there you'll be given further orders. I just want to let you guys know that we've had incoming from Charlie tonight, so, if the sirens blow and you are outside, try to find some cover. If you're on the buses and we come under attack, hit the floor, and cover your face, to protect it from flying glass. Now, get your gear and move out."

Jim said, "You got to be kidding me. Like you said earlier Bob, there isn't anywhere safe in this country."

Bob looked at Jim with a small smile and joked, "If I were you, I'd volunteer to join me in the jungles. At least I will be hunting Charlie instead of waiting around for him to get me or have a mortar or rocket drop on my head."

"No way!" said Jim, "I'll take my chances in the rear. I'll make sure I have a strong lock on my door to keep Charlie out. The way I read in the papers and saw on TV; Nixon is trying to get us out of this place. He's supposed to order men out of here to show the public that he's trying to find an honorable way to end this war. A lot of people back home are against us being here."

"I know," said Bob, "One of the reasons I broke up with my girlfriend is because she wanted me to desert to Canada and marry her. There is no way I'm ready to marry anyone plus, I couldn't run from my responsibility to my country by not fighting in Vietnam. I'm not really that worried about being here."

"You are a real fool," said Jim. "Anyone who isn't worried about fighting in Nam must have his head examined."

"Yeah, maybe you are right but something inside is directing me so whatever happens, happens," answered Bob.

"Well, I wish you luck Bob since there is no turning back now," Bill said.

The replacements were in no hurry to leave the security of the plane. They shuffled out slowly to the new world awaiting them.

None knew their fate or if they would ever return to the states, that but for only a few hours earlier, provided them safety. All would have to at least spend a year in a country torn by war. All were on day one of a three hundred sixty-five-day tour that some would survive, some would not, and all would be influenced and **scarred for life**. None would return the same man, as when they arrived.

Finally, with only the few personal items plus his newly issued jungle fatigues, Bob began the long walk to the door: to begin an adventure that would affect him for the rest of his life and was in his blood. He was a survivor, a fighter, a warrior, smart enough to rely on his instincts and the forces within that directed him. Afraid he was, but also inquisitive to find out what lie ahead.

He was anxious to begin his tour, to get his year over, to fight in the jungles, to accept the responsibilities of survival, and to get back home to his family, alive: he was confident in his abilities, the toughness of his mind, his determination, and his resilience to succeed.

So, Bob moved on, used all of his natural survival instincts and senses to prepare him for the unknown. As he moved closer to the door, he felt the heat of the night and the smell of the jet fuel. But, he still wasn't prepared for the blast of heat, nostril-burning smell of jet fuel, and noise that hit him as he stepped from the plane into the night.

A tall redheaded flight attendant that flashed a big smile at the men as they filed passed her, was at the door to wish the men luck. Bob took her hand and then pulled her to him for a hug; both knew she may be the last American woman he may ever see.

Bob thought of his family and his promise he made to his twin brother, a promise to his identical twin that he would be home for his wedding in July to be his best man. Thinking of his loneliness, the thought of knowing no one, so little about the country, its people, or what challenges lie ahead, all caused tears to build up in his eyes. He missed his family and his twin brother. He made his family and his promise the heart of his drive for survival. They would be the main reason not to give up, to do more than necessary or required, and try to maintain as much control of his destiny as possible.

The solitude and isolation he felt, even with hundreds of men around, and the second-guessing whether he should have deserted, was overwhelming. Bob had not gotten used to the helplessness of others directing his life, the fact of not knowing what to expect, and what lie ahead. He was totally alone. Bill and Jim were the only ones Bob knew and he had just met them while flying to Vietnam.

He knew that in most other wars whole units were shipped overseas and fought together. Each man knew the other but, on this flight, all were strangers. Each man was given orders and traveled on their own to their new assignments. None knew where they would spend their tour or with what unit they would fight. By the time Bob reached the bottom of the steps and took his first steps into a country that was covered with young American's blood, he was in control of his thoughts and emotions, ready for whatever lie ahead.

As Bob followed Bill and Jim to the buses, some of the men, waiting to return home, called out to wish them luck. One of the guys, wearing the blue braid of Army infantry on his right shoulder, walked over, and grabbed Bob's hand to shake it. He was tan and stood about five-ten with short wavy blonde hair. Below his nose was a short well-groomed mustache that matched the color of his hair. He looked old, older than what Bob thought was his age and had a look in his eyes, a look that Bob had seen in wild animals.

He smiled at Bob shaking his hand saying, "My name is Harry Slamer, from Parks, Indiana. I see you are infantry. I want to wish you luck, it's not easy out there. My advice to you is to carry plenty of ammo, keep your head down, and don't take any drugs when out in the boonies. I saw too many guys high on some bad shit and it made them wild. A few even got killed for no reason, it's hard enough straight, let alone high."

"That is no problem," said Bob, "I don't take drugs. By the way, what unit were you with?"

"I was with the Second and Tenth Charlie Company Twenty-Fifth Infantry Division, a real good unit. The Twenty-Fifth took a lot of shit back in the 68 Tet but the action is not too bad now. You still run into a few VC once in a while or find a few tunnels," answered Harry.

Bob thanked him and wanted to ask more questions but the buses pulled up and the new arrivals began to board them.

Jim jokingly said, as they moved single file to board the buses, "Dam Bob, maybe I should be infantry the kind of respect you get."

Bob just smiled as he thought back to his Advanced Infantry Training. He realized then that drugs would cause him to be a loner. In a letter to his family, he wrote how he couldn't get over the number of drugs that were there: almost everyone was getting high. He had no one to hang around with and nowhere to go.

The drugs started with some of the guys getting high on weekend leave. Then it progressed to a point where most of the guys were getting high and a few were even getting high during the week for training.

Being the leader of the Delta A R platoon, Bob tried to stop it for fear of someone getting hurt. Finally, one of the guys named Pat asked Bob to get high on coke. He was sitting around with four other guys and they were talking about going to get high, he asked, "Come on Bob, you want to get high? You feel like you can do anything on this stuff. Everyone else is doing it so what the hell. We're going to Vietnam anyway, so what is the difference if we have a good time before we go?"

Bob's jaw tightened, he inhaled slowly, then turned from one guy to the next challenging each, and said, "I've known for some time that you guys have been getting high and I really don't give two shits what anyone does on the weekend. But, during the week, while we're training, I better not catch anyone getting high. If you guys keep getting high during training, I'm going to report you to the sergeant. You know, goddamn it, how important it is to be ready and learn as much as we can. Most of these guys, like Gillette, are only in for six months. They're only weekend warriors and they don't have to worry about fighting or being killed like us. Besides, there's no way I need that white dream dust. If I'm going to Nam, I want to make sure I'm straight so I can get back home. So, don't ever try to talk me into getting high again. OK, come on you guys, you don't need this shit either."

"You are right," replied Pat. "Most of those other guys are only here for six months, they're not going to Nam. Come on let's go have a few beers."

48

A drop of sweat slipped into Bob's eye causing it to burn. It was hot, the sweat was already beading up on his forehead, and his army fatigues became saturated with the moistness that covered his body to cool him. He moved forward slowly to learn as much as possible about his surroundings, and to look for cover in case they were shelled. He was amazed at the amount of activity. There were men everywhere, working, standing around, or just walking in every direction, as if it was the middle of the afternoon, not 0200 hours in the morning.

Jets were taking off or landing. Every once in a while, F-5 Freedom Fighter jets taxied to the runway and in the distance, helicopters could be heard taking off.

Bob thought of his family. In Basic and Advanced Infantry Training he always tried to imagine what his family and friends were doing. He would find himself doing it more often being more homesick, living under the fear of death, and much farther away

It was the thirteenth of December in Vietnam so it was about 1300 hours, the twelfth of December at home. He imagined that everyone would be getting ready for Christmas. Since he would not be home for Christmas, his family and friends gave him a pre-Christmas party.

Everyone tried to be in the Christmas spirit, but all had Vietnam hanging over them. Bob's mother was at the verge of crying throughout the whole party, always with tissues in her hand, wiping away tears every time he received a gift. Bob received gifts from every family member.

His twin gave him a watch, the first watch he had ever owned. It was a silver band Timex that gave the time and date. His twin brother handed it to Bob saying, "I hope you can use it, if not I'll take it back.

"The watch was wrapped in silver wrapping paper with green Christmas trees. Bob had no idea what it was so he opened it slowly not wanting to rip the paper.

The whole family sat quietly, they must have known what it was and they were waiting for his response. Realizing it was a watch, water collected in Bob's eyes while he looked at his own reflection in his twin. He reached out and hugged his twin asking,

"How did you know I wanted a watch? You don't know how much I need one." It was only natural for them to share thoughts.

The younger kids gave him drawings or something that they thought would be used while in Nam. All the gifts had to be returned except the watch.

Bob planned to use the watch as inspiration. He knew that every time he looked at his watch it would remind him of his family, and his twin.

"Boy is it hot in this bus," one of the guys complained as he got on the bus. "It's like an oven." "You'd better get used to this heat because it is cool now compared to how hot it gets during the day. You can cook an egg in the sun and it gets so humid, you can almost drink the air. Just open a couple windows if you find any that open. It will cool a little when we get moving," said the driver.

"Come on Bob we'll sit in the back. It should get cooler in a little bit," said Bill. "You know this bus looks like it's been here forever. I wonder how it's still running? Damn, it's hot in here."

"Do you really think they received incoming, or was the guy on the plane trying to scare us?" asked Bill.

Bob called out to the driver, "Did you really have some incoming tonight?"

"Hell no!" laughed the driver. "They always tell the newcomers that to scare them. We haven't had any incoming for about a week, and that was only a few mortars that hit the outer parts of the base. Things have really cooled off lately. Last March the Viet Cong sappers crawled through the minefields and barbed wire and blew up fourteen CH-47 Chinook helicopters at the main 25th headquarters at Cu Chi. This whole Summer and Fall, Charlie have kept to the outer bush. They really got their ass kicked in 68 during their Tet Offensive. We really beat the shit out of them". Ref. 3

"Yeah, we kicked their ass but we lost a lot of our men doing it," responded Bob.

"That's why Nixon is pulling out some of our guys. He wants to try to end this thing before more are lost," explained the driver.

The idea of the war ending made Bob feel as if there was hope. The President, Congress, and a good portion of the American people wanted to end the war so, there was always a chance the war would be over before the end of his tour.

The problem was, Hanoi knew that it was just a matter of time before the United States would have to stop fighting, since the country was being torn apart over the war. Ho Chi Minh knew that if they just hung in there and continued to send dead Americans home, eventually, they would win the war.

Bob tried his best when writing home not to let his family know how scared and homesick he was. The day he left the states, just a few hours earlier, he had sent a letter wishing them a Merry Christmas. He told them that the worst thing about being away is not being with them on Christmas.

This was his first Christmas he would not spend with his family that enjoyed and celebrated Christmas in the old-fashioned way, with a live Christmas tree, lights, and wrapped packages around the tree. Everyone opened presents, so no matter what each received, there were always a mass of gifts with a family of nine children. Oh, how he will miss the singing and the joy on his younger brother's and sisters' faces as they opened their presents.

The buses in front began to move out. It was dark and hard to see as Bob looked out the windows trying to get an idea what the country was like. It took about ten minutes to get to the barracks. Once there, the men were told to move into the barracks and find a bunk. None of the bunks had sheets or pillows. The mattresses were old and rolled up, but no one seemed to care.

Bob hung with Bill and Jim since they were the only ones he knew. They rolled down the mattresses and were ready to lie down when a big muscular man walked up to Bill and said, "Hey man, this is my bunk go find another."

Bill wasn't going to argue since this mountain of a man towered over him by at least six inches, and started to move to another bunk. Bob asked, "Hey Bill what's wrong? Is this guy bothering you?"

Bob was tired, in no mood, and he didn't like his friend being pushed around. He had also learned long ago to establish himself as quickly as he could. The big man turned slowly to face Bob, looking down with muscles bulging and said, "What's the problem with you, little white boy? Why don't you stay out of this here thing before I break you in two?"

Before he finished, Bob moved like a flash, threw a lightning fast left to the man's gut, and followed with a right cross to the left jaw. The force of the blow sent Bob's first casualty of the war flying into the wall with such force the whole barracks shook. Then very slowly the passed-out bully slid to the floor like a big rag doll. Everyone in the barracks stood shocked not believing what they just saw and how fast it was over.

Bill smiled and said, "Bob did you see that guy trip and fall, I wonder if he's all right? He better watch where he's walking." Then quietly said to Bob, "I can't believe you put that guy down so fast. I thought he was going to kick your ass. I would have given him my bunk."

Sitting down on his bunk, Bob said, "Since I'm here in this godforsaken country, there's no way I'm letting anyone push me or my friends around. It's bad enough I have to take orders from my superiors let alone take shit from anyone else. Now, let's get this guy to a bunk and get some sleep.

Robert M. Braun, Sr.

New Day

The sun was just beginning to show its light over the Eastern horizon when I stirred from the dirty, well-used bunk. The springs were strained from the many bodies that have passed through this unfriendly far away country, and slept upon it. It brought back memories of the time when I was young, when I roomed with my brothers and slept on bunk beds that were used when my parents purchased them. Sleeping on the top bunk, which sagged in the middle, I would roll over the edge and drop onto my twin brother's bed. How I missed my twin, and family.

Fully clothed, I rose to face my first full day in Vietnam. There was a chorus of snoring from the men in the barracks, all exhausted from the trip. I moved quietly to the bunk of the man that fell victim to my sting the night before: seeing him snoring, fast asleep in the same position where he was laid, reassured me that no permanent harm had been done.

Outside the oranges and the yellows were but a thin sliver on the horizon, that gave way to the grays, and then the blackness of what was left of the night. The air was still, and there was a touch of heat that woke the many sweat pores of my body.

As I peered out the door, I saw the black silhouettes of other unkempt barracks in a line alongside my barrack. In front of the row of barracks ran a dirt road that joined a paved road.

I looked at my Timex, instantly thought of my twin and family, wondering what they were doing. It was 0525 hours and almost time for the other men to be brought back from their dreams. At that moment a spec-six walked into the barrack to awaken the new arrivals. He was surprised to see me awake asking,

"Didn't sleep too well?" looking at me with a friendly smile.

"I slept OK but I'm anxious to find out what this country is like," I responded as I walked toward the spec-six hoping I could talk to him to find out what was going to happen. When close enough I stretched out my right hand for a handshake. The spec-six took my hand and shook vigorously saying,

"My name is Tom Billings from Pittsburgh, glad to meet you." "I'm Bob Braun, Pittsburgh, we're almost neighbors. I'm from Washington Crossing, New Jersey."

"Jersey, no shit. How was the weather back home? The way I've heard it's pretty cold. It's a lot different here, always hot as hell," said Tom quietly.

"Yeah, when I left New Jersey it was really cold and they were talking about a white Christmas," I answered. "By the way, what's going to happen today?"

"Come on Bob, help me wake these guys up, so they can get ready to go to the mess hall for breakfast. After breakfast, some of you guys will join a convoy that runs from Saigon to Cu Chi, while others will be sent to other division headquarters throughout Nam," explained the spec-six. "It will take about an hour or so to reach Cu Chi by the convoy. Anyone not going to Cu Chi will be flown to their division headquarters."

It was 0735 hours when the trucks moved out towards the main entrance of Tan Son Nhut Air Base, bellowing out thick black diesel smoke from their exhaust, that drifted back towards the men standing in the back of the trucks. Even this early in the morning, the air was thick with moisture that caused sweat to sit on the skin. I knew my body would adjust to the climate so, I was not bothered by the heat.

Looking from the open back of the truck I could see there was a line of six trucks, with jeep escort. Outside the gate, Route 1 was clogged with traffic of all kinds, from ox-drawn carts, to a long line of a truck convoy that we were to join.

The air was filled with the acidity stench of thick black diesel exhaust. The sound of heavy truck engines made it almost impossible to hear the man next to you. Overhead, helicopter gunships flew to protect the convoy, adding to the noise.

Bill, who stood next to me yelled, "Bob I saw you talking to the guy you decked last night. Wasn't he mad at you?"

"No," I answered. "Matter of fact he told me that he had never been knocked out by anyone before and he said he was the heavyweight Golden Glove Champ of New York a couple of years before being drafted into the Army. He said he would have turned pro, but, got in trouble with drugs."

"No shit," said an impressed Bill. "I tell you I've seen a lot of fights but I have never seen anyone faster or hit harder than you."

"Thanks, I had to learn how to fight to protect myself against my brothers."

Once part of the convoy to Cu Chi, the trucks moved slowly along Route 1. All traffic was stopped to allow the convoy to move through, unstopped. At every intersection the Vietnamese people stood and watched the convoy.

I studied the people and the land: surprised at their small thin size and the way they packed every moving vehicle. Small cars had people hanging on the outside because there was no room inside. A number of the buildings were nothing but shells with four walls that were marked with machine gun bullet holes. Burned out trucks and other vehicles littered the sides of Route 1, evidence of past battles.

"Look at that," said Bill, "I can't believe that many people can fit on that small car. There must be fifteen people in and hanging on it. I wonder how the damn thing can move?"

"Shit Bill, I bet the car and all the people don't weigh over a thousand pounds," I laughed. "I don't know what these people eat but they all look like they're starving, they're so small and thin. Hey look at those girls over there, goddamn, they're beautiful."

Alongside the road were five girls all wearing black pajama pants with a light-colored pullover called Ao BaBa. Their long straight midnight black hair hung down to the middle of their backs, tall and thin waving to the soldiers, with big bright pearly white smiles. The new arrivals waved back not realizing that these very same innocent beauties, may someday confront them on the battlefield. All of the new warriors were all wide-eyed, sucking up all the sights of this new dangerous country.

Cu Chi Base Camp Entrance

Robert M. Braun, Sr.

Short History of **"The Bob Hope Christmas Show"**

Bob Hope started recording an episode for the NBC Radio Show on May 1941 to begin a decades-long tradition of providing entertainment for our Military Service Members.

His first overseas trip was the USO Show in 1943 followed by many more WWII shows that featured many of the biggest names in Hollywood. The shows for WWII made him loved by many service members and families. Bob began hosting "The Bob Hope Christmas Show" in the mid-twentieth Century.

Christmas Shows, USO Trips and Vietnam

In 1964 Bob hosted nine USO trips in Vietnam. Over the years "The Bob Hope Christmas Show" included such stars and celebrities as Ann-Margret, Lola Falana, Raquel Welch, Rosie Grier, Neil Armstrong, Sammy Davis, Jr., as well as other lesser-known acts, comedians, singers, and dance troupes, such as TV's "Golddiggers."

Many of us that were lucky enough to see the show feel it was one of the highlights of our time in Vietnam. It was one of the highlights of my tour. I can still remember singing "Silent Night" at the end of the show with Bob Hope, Connie Stevens, Neil Armstrong, the other stars, and all the other Vietnam Veterans at the show. The memory still brings tears to my eyes.

I also remember writing home about the show I attended at the Cu Chi 25th Infantry Division Headquarters, on December 23rd, 1969. I wrote to tell my family that I was at the show and that I was one of the guys without a shirt. A few weeks later I received a letter from my Mother telling me the whole family sat and watched the show, looking for me but, couldn't find me in the crowd because almost all the men watching the show had no shirts.

My family, like the many other families, watched the show hoping to catch a glimpse of their loved one serving in Vietnam. The Bob Hope 1970 Christmas specials are among the most popular television specials of all time. The last Bob Hope Christmas Show in Vietnam was in 1972.

Bob Hope said: *"I hope I can be excused a little sentimentality as I look back over 22 of these Christmas trips [and remember] the millions of service men and women who responded to our efforts with warmth, enthusiasm and affection." Ref. 4*

The Bob Hope Christmas Show

The show was held on December 23rd, 1969 at the 25th Infantry Division base Cu Chi. The base is/was located on Highway 1 about 25k from Tan Son Nhut Air Base. **This was the air base I was flown into a few days prior to the performance.**

The base and the 25th were there to protect Saigon from attacks from the VC (Viet Cong) and NVA (North Vietnam Army) coming from Cambodia into War Zone C. **It was located just south of the Viet Cong stronghold, the Iron Triangle, and over the Cu Chi tunnels. Ref. 5**

I had tunnels training the day before and was surprised that there were thousands of miles of tunnels in, around, under Cu Chi, and throughout Vietnam. The tunnels were begun in the 1880s to resist French occupation. They were further expanded after the French War, later U.S. backed South Vietnamese government, and were especially concentrated around and under Cu Chi, right where I was stationed.

I was told a story about the problems securing the area around Cu Chi during Operation Crimp in 1966. Even in a tight defensive perimeter, casualties continued to mount from random Viet Cong attacks. The VC would appear and disappear, like magic. At dusk on January 11th, 1966, suddenly there were several grenade explosions and rifle fire. As soldiers were relaxing, a VC popped out of a trap door and threw two grenades, and sprayed the area with rifle fire, then dropped down and shut the trap door.

These are pictures of a tunnel under Cu Chi, and trap doors the VC used to surprise soldiers in the field: one that is closed, and the other open.

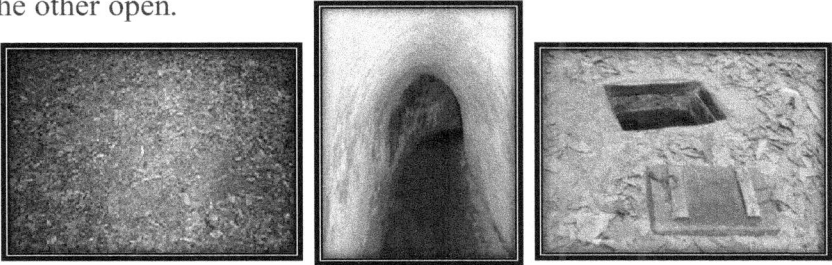

Also, I was told (and saw the broadcast on national television) March 10th, 1969, only nine months before, Cu Chi was attacked by the Viet Cong sapper squads, that slipped undetected through the barbed wire perimeter defense, and placed explosives on the giant Chinook helicopters, destroying nine and damaging four others.

I learned about the tunnels the day before guarding the stage for "The Bob Hope Christmas Show", in an area called the Lightning Bowl. Neil Armstrong, Rosey Grier, Les Brown and His Band of Renown, Linda Bennett, The Golddiggers, Kelly Hope, 1968 Miss World, Penelope Plummer-Melbourne, Australia, and Connie Stevens, along with Bob Hope, were in the show.

As I look back on this, I remember being afraid, but under control, and on high alert. Over the years I have shown acts of bravery by being the first to dive off a ten-foot diving board, as well as crawling under the house for dead rats. Just the thought of being in a war zone for only a short time, learning about the tunnels, the amount of fighting still going on, and knowing how important "The Bob Hope Christmas Show" was; I was even told that the VC knew about the show, and may try to stop it, still sends shivers down my spine.

Bob Hope and the other entertainers had to travel in a safety pod of three aircraft to fly into Cu Chi, and Bob Hope noted, *"Every time we come here, there is action!"*

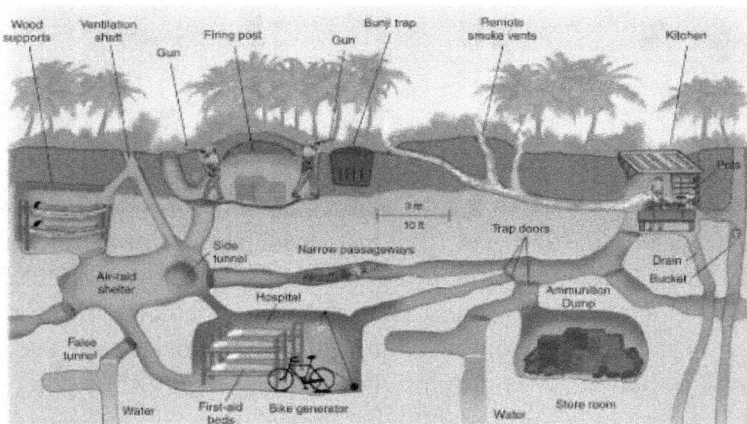

I had watched the action of the war in Vietnam, almost every night on TV, and saw the fighting during the 1968 Tet, and the March 10th, 1969, attack on Cu Chi.

I knew I was most likely heading there because of that night after a basketball game, in my senior year of high school, I had a dream, a nightmare, where I saw myself in a firefight in Vietnam.

Over the last few days, I was assigned a M-16, had M-16 training, guard duty, spent some off time swimming in the large inground pool, and almost gotten used to the hot weather.

The day before the show, I reported for guard duty with my helmet, M-16, and flight jacket. I was then driven with a few other men to the area of the stage for the show.

The night was warm and clear. It had been another hot day, and I made sure I had a lot of insect repellent because the mosquitoes were going to be out in full force. There wasn't quite a full moon, but close to it. I remember saying and thinking to myself to stay in the shadows, something I did a lot of growing up. Many summer nights my brothers, sisters, and the kids in the neighborhood played hide and go seek. I spent many nights walking to friends' houses at night. So, I was used to being invisible at night.

The Lightning Bowl was a large area built like a half bowl, with the stage at the front. There was enough room for thousands of men that would be there the next day, and I would be one of them.

The first thing I did was check out the area I was to guard that night and find a few places where I could watch, but not be seen. I patrolled out in the seating area, up on the stage, and all around the back of the stage, and found a few spots where I could stay out of sight but, still remain in contact with the other men guarding the area.

At first there were a lot of guys checking out the Lightning Bowl and stage but, as the night moved on, things got quiet.

I remember looking up to the almost full moon thinking of Neil Armstrong stepping off the ladder saying, *"One small step for man: one giant leap for mankind"*, when he became the first human to walk on the Moon.

My whole company was called into the rec room to watch the landing and history be made. I had been in basic training for only one week, so, it was quite a treat, since I had been closely following the space exploration growing up.

I remember watching the TV back in 1961 when it was reported that the Soviet Union launched the first satellite to circle the earth, and was one of the record number of people watching Apollo 8, the first manned mission to enter lunar orbit on Christmas Eve, December 24th, 1968, about a year before.

I thought back to President Kennedy's speech, when announcing the United States is going to the moon, *"We choose to go to the Moon in this decade and do the other things, not because they are easy, but because they are hard."* So, knowing that I would be seeing Neil Armstrong the next day, was really exciting.

As the night moved on, I began to think about where I was last year at this time. My high school basketball team had just completed playing a Christmas Tournament, where I had a great game, to help our small school beat the sixth ranked team in the state of New Jersey. I can still see the large headlines on the back page of a local paper the next day saying, "Giant Killers Hopewell Valley". We ended up coming in second place in the tournament, against three much larger schools.

Later that year, I remember being in Washington, D.C. on my senior class trip, when Martin Luther King was assassinated on April 4th, 1968 in Memphis, Tennessee. The next day, we were to visit the Washington, D. C. Zoo.

Since I was already nineteen and legal to drink in D. C., I would sneak away and have a few drinks in local bars. Once we got to the zoo, a friend and I grabbed a cab and went to a bar. While there, we saw on TV that riots were happening and they were closing down the city, so we knew we had to get back to the zoo.

Once outside, the roads were filled with cars evacuating D. C. and, smoke from burning buildings could be seen in the distance. We made it back to the zoo after jumping into a car driven by a girl who said she was going by the zoo.

No one was in the zoo since it was closed because of the riots. We finally made it back to the buses, after being found, and told by security guards that they had been looking for us for the last two hours. All the other students were on the buses waiting for us. We were both feeling pretty good so, it was obvious we were drinking. We were suspended from all school activities and not allowed to leave a teacher's side for the rest of the trip.

I was homesick, and still had almost a year to go on my one-year tour. This was the first Christmas I would be away and not spending it with my family. Over the years, my whole family had watched "The Bob Hope Christmas Show", and I couldn't believe I was guarding the stage for his show in a war zone, half the world away from my home.

The night moved slowly on and I couldn't stop thinking about home, which I did a lot while in Nam. My home was near the Delaware River where George Washington crossed on that cold snowy Christmas night on America's way to freedom. I had grown up in the Crossing, and worked during the summers while in high school at Washington Crossing State Park, New Jersey. So, I knew the hardship the soldiers went through on that night, and was hoping to use their courage and determination to help me to survive Vietnam.

This is a picture of the Washington Crossing Bridge that

connects New Jersey and Pennsylvania, looking from the Jersey side to where Washington and his men crossed.

This is the famous picture by Emanuel Leutze that I saw a number of times growing up.

Since, I knew I was going to Vietnam, I had worked hard while in Basic and Advanced Infantry Training. While at Basic, I was expert in all my weapons training, and ended up being the outstanding trainee of my Basic Training cycle, having the highest combined physical and academic scores. Another thing I had going for me: I was used to being in the woods and forest around my home and knew how to read tracks and move without making noise.

At this time, I did not know where I would be heading but, would receive my orders in the next day or two. I just wanted to get through the night so, I was on high alert. Every half hour I would patrol around the stage area and would slip from one dark area to the other. All was quiet.

The night dragged on, finally the eastern sky began to brighten showing the signs of another day. I can remember not being tired, and couldn't wait to see the show and write home about it.

Robert M. Braun, Sr.

Christmas and New Year's Eve

On the 24th of December 1969 I received my orders. I was assigned to the 2nd Battalion, 12th Infantry, 25th Infantry Division, Bravo Company, 1st Platoon, 1st Squad. From the Welcome Center, also known as Cu Chi Hilton Hotel, I moved to the 2nd and 12th headquarters in Cu Chi, where I would spend a few days, until I would be trucked out to FSB Pershing.

FSB Pershing was started the first week of October 1968. The base was oddly shaped with its east and south borders measuring about 800 feet and the north border about 1,200 feet. It was the home of the 2nd and 12th Infantry Battalion and B Battery 7th and 8th Artillery. The base was there to supply artillery support for men out in the field and the infantry was there to protect the artillery, along with patrolling the area and setting up night ambushes.

The fire support bases were combined infantry-artillery positions that sometimes-included armor. Depending on the planned duration of the position, firebases could be dug-in heavily and reinforced with engineer assets. Perhaps the greatest strength of the firebases was their ability to cover each other with mutually supporting artillery fire over great distances. It is a long-standing principle of firepower that massing fires is the most effective way to use artillery. Ref. 6

The headquarters in Cu Chi was used to supply the soldiers at FSB Pershing with the needs of hundreds of men stationed there. It had a small building: one room with a few desks and another with cots for sleeping.

To my surprise there was a small dirt basketball court with a ten-foot basket. I was able to shoot a few baskets with a couple of the guys.

There wasn't much for me to do since my in-country training was completed so, I helped pack the supplies that were shipped daily to FSB Pershing and anything else to help the guys there. I was able to spend some time at the inground swimming pool and go to the big PX. I was working on a real good tan.

At night I would join a few guys at the NCO Club (Non-commissioned Officers Club) where we had a few beers and listened to music, and that is where I spent Christmas Eve; my first time I would not be with my family.

During the night I continued to look down at the watch my twin gave me at an early Christmas party before heading to Vietnam. I was thirteen hours ahead, so I knew everyone at was most likely most likely getting ready for Christmas.

I was sitting by myself sipping my beer, thinking. I drifted back to the day I was drafted and not my twin brother. We traveled to Newark, New Jersey on a bus together and both had our physicals; I passed, Rich didn't. Just before I was given my oath and sworn into the Army, my twin waved goodbye. He was heading home and I was being sent to Fort Dix, New Jersey for Basic Training, then Fort Lewis, Washington for Advanced Infantry Training, and now, in Vietnam.

He failed the physical because of an injury he received when we were in fifth grade; my twin had an accident that almost took off his left hand. We were at the Pennington Prep School, Pennington, New Jersey during a football game one Saturday. Our father was refereeing the game.

We ended up playing football behind the bleachers against two kids from the neighborhood. We were doing pretty well, holding our own. I was the quarterback. My twin hiked the ball to me and broke right toward the bleachers. He made a good catch and ended up being tackled right behind the bleachers. Rich screamed and stood up; blood shot out of his left hand. He landed on a broken Coke bottle that almost cut off his left hand.

Luckily, a fan in the bleachers jumped down and applied pressure to try to stop the bleeding. I was terrified, but didn't panic, and went to him to help. The front of Rich's shirt was covered with blood. I was told to run up to the nurse's station to alert them of my brother's injuries. I ran as fast as I could. When Rich got to the nurse's station they applied a temporary bandage, continued to apply pressure, and called for the ambulance.

I can still hear the sirens blasting calling the ambulance. Unable to do anything, I ran onto the football field in the middle of the game, to tell our dad Rich was hurt badly and would be taken to the hospital.

It didn't take long for the ambulance to arrive. They put Rich into the ambulance with his hand bandaged and I followed. We were rushed to the hospital, sirens blasting the whole way.

While I was in the waiting room, I couldn't help the tears and I couldn't sit down. One of the nurses saw I was alone and how upset I was, and came over to console me. I told her about my twin; how badly he had been hurt. She bought me a soda, gave me a hug, assured me that everything would be ok. It helped.

My mother and father finally arrived and I was able to tell them that Rich was in recovery with a ton of stitches holding his left hand together. My father went to the nurse's station to ask about Rich. We eventually were able to visit Rich, his left hand wrapped with a lot of bandages.

Rich took a while to heal, his ring finger and pinkie were crippled and it is why he got out of being drafted into the Army.

Being drafted into the Army and sent to Vietnam was the first time away from my twin for an extended period. What helped me handle being alone was, my twin and I were sent to different schools at the end of fourth grade. I had to learn to be on my own without my twin at my side. This helped me spend my first Christmas without my twin and family and would help me survive the jungles of Vietnam.

A bunch of guys were in the NCO Club and Christmas music was playing. The club had a Christmas tree with decorations and Christmas lights hung around the room. There were a couple of tables set up with all kinds of finger foods. After a few beers, we all joined in singing Christmas songs. The one we sang loudest was, "I'll Be Home for Christmas".

Another song that hit home was "Silent Night". I instantly flashed back to "The Bob Hope Christmas Show"; at the end of the show Bob Hope, Connie Stevens, Neil Armstrong, the other stars, and over three thousand other Vietnam Veterans, including me, that were there, joined in to sing the song.

I couldn't help a few tears along with a bunch of other guys. It was the first Christmas most of us would not be home, away in a country thousands of miles from home.

We all tried to be in the Christmas spirit but, we were in Vietnam. The next few days flew by and on December 28th, 1969, I was on my way to my unit. I rode shotgun in a jeep as part of a convoy that traveled from Cu Chi everyday twenty-three miles on a dusty dirt road with all kinds of traffic, from tanks to oxen carts. We traveled in a long line with enough distance between the vehicles to let the dust clear and not be too close in case of incoming.

I sat in an open jeep as shotgun with my M-16 on my lap and a bunch of magazines. We didn't have as many trucks and jeeps as we had when I was taken from Tan Son Nhut Air Force Base to Cu Chi but it was a strong force with a few helicopters flying overhead. Ref. 7

As we traveled, I studied the landscape and terrain, trying to see what type of country where I would be fighting.

The land was flat and very dry. It was the beginning of the dry season and it looked like it.

In the distance there were hedgerows. Rice fields that were surrounded by dikes were on both sides of the road. Some of the paddies were green from irrigation with women working in them. The women didn't even look up from their work, accustomed to the convoys that pass by every day.

Just before leaving Cu Chi, I was told by the guys at the 2nd and 12th headquarters, that it was a long ride and to be ready just in case. They told me I was assigned to a real good unit, Bravo Company, 1st Platoon, 1st Squad. Some considered it the best squad in the company. They told me about the last new guy, almost two weeks ago, that was assigned to the unit, a guy named Jack Rae Smith from Iowa. I told them I would look him up.

It took a couple hours to reach FSB Pershing. At the main gate there was a tall twenty-five foot well-fortified tower. Since the area was flat you could see a long way from the top.

Around the bunkers were row after row of barbed wire with what looked like fifty gallon barrels scattered between the wire. Throughout the wire were trip flares. Later I found out the fifty gallon barrels were filled with napalm.

Napalm is an incendiary mixture of a gelling agent and a volatile petrochemical usually gasoline or diesel fuel, thickened with special soaps. Ref. 8

There were bunkers around just inside the barbed wire that were used for guard duty at night and in the middle were five 105 howitzers, mortar pits, and a number of hooches. The well fortified hooches were built with dirt filled ammo boxes with sandbags on top.

There were a couple large tents that were used as a mess hall and kitchen, with areas of wooden outhouses with places to shower next to them.

Once inside FSB Pershing, I was directed to where the Bravo Company, 1st Platoon, 1st Squad was located. When I got there, I was greeted by a few guys. The squad had just gotten back from a four-day mission and wouldn't be going out for a few days. One of the guys was, Jack Smith.

He greeted me with a smile and a handshake. Jack was about five foot ten with light brown hair. He had an athletic

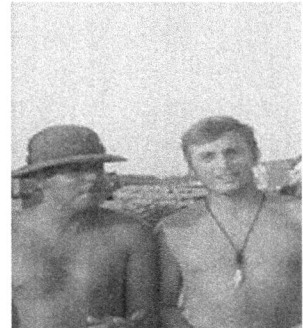

Lopez   Jack

body and had a strong grip. You could tell he played some kind of sport. Along with Jack I met some of the other guys named Brownie, Lopez, Pusher, and Tennessee.

After telling the guys a little about myself, Jack took me to meet our platoon leader, Lieutenant Sparks. Lieutenant Sparks was thin, about six foot tall with blonde hair. After I saluted him, he greeted me with a smile and handshake and said he had been told I would be joining his platoon. After spending some time telling Lieutenant Sparks about myself, I carried my gear into the hooch that would be my home while in FSB Pershing that I would share with Jack, Brownie, and Lopez.

The M-79 was given to me the first day I arrived at FSB Pershing when I had to turn over my M-16 to, what turned out to be my best friend and future fellow point man, Jack Rae Smith. He had been in country a little less than two weeks prior to my arrival and was happy to get my M-16. It was a policy to give the M-79 to new members of the unit.

The M-79 was effective against a wide range of targets from personnel to light armored vehicles. It could be used to  fire a number of different rounds that included: high explosive anti-personnel grenade, smoke, buckshot, and illumination rounds. Ref. 9

I had watched on the news the Battle of Hamburger Hill (13–20 May 1969) during Operation Apache and saw that some units ran out of ammo and remembered that the guy at the airport, Harry Slamer, had advised me to carry a lot of ammo. So, I always made sure I carried more than was required. When I exchanged my M-16 for the M-79, Jack gave me the biggest smile, and was surprised about how many M-16 magazines I was carrying. I told him why, he agreed with me, and said he carried more ammo than recommended, as well.

For the next few days, I hung around the guys to get to know them, had a few beers, and had no problem sleeping on the hard wooden bunk beds inside the hooch. At night I spent an hour on watch in the bunkers surrounding FSB Pershing with one of the other guys.

On the morning of the thirty-first, New Year's Eve, we received orders that we would be heading out at dusk on a night ambush. Around an hour before dusk, we were ready to move out. I had my M-79 loaded with a high explosive round and was in the middle of the line. This was the first time since I was in Vietnam that I would be on patrol on a night ambush. We exited FSB Pershing through its main gate past the sign that warned us about mosquitoes.

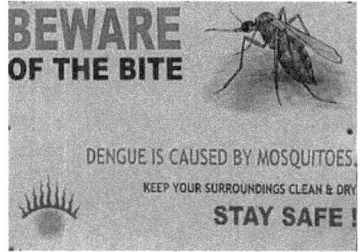

I was surprised I wasn't scared but on high alert walking between Lopez and Jack. We didn't go far outside the wire and set up near the firebase's dump. It was the practice of the VC to come to the dump at night to see if they could find something useful.

The warm night dragged by with two men on for an hour watch while the rest slept. I didn't sleep too much that first night on ambush and would get used to night ambushes in a very short time. I learned that first night to have a supply of mosquito repellent with me.

It was a New Year's Eve that, I will never forget!

A few night ambushes later I got to see my first dead Viet Cong soldier. The second squad of my platoon killed a Viet Cong walking on a dike where they had set up their ambush. Because Jack and I were new, we were taken to where the dead VC was located, to see a dead body.

It wasn't nice. The body was twisted, the back of his head was blown off, and his brain was scattered on the weeds around the head. What surprised me the most was the small hole in the front of the head caused the entire back of the head to be blown off. This wouldn't be the last dead body I would see.

I found out later that the M-16 bullet was small and traveled at a high speed. When it hit something like an arm or head, the bullet tumbled, causing much more damage. This made the M-16 a deadly weapon that was light and easy to carry. I can understand why Jack was happy, and gave me that big smile, when he got my M-16.

Robert M. Braun, Sr.

This is my first article about Vietnam that was published in a national magazine in the late 1990s.

THE SUN AT LAST

The night of January 5th, 1970 has left an impression that still affects my life today. I still remember watching the bombing and smelling the sulfur that filled the air, wondering how many NVA were killed or injured, feeling lonely, and thinking about my family back in the states asleep in their warm secure homes.

I was an inexperienced 20-year-old country boy who grew up playing sports and exploring the fields and woods around my home. I was the third of nine children, and I had rarely been away from home without a family member. I flew for the first time when shipped out to Fort Lewis, Washington after Basic Training. After only two months of Basic Training and two months of Advanced Infantry Training and only six months in the Army, I was alone in Vietnam, stationed with the 2nd Battalion, 12th Infantry, 25th Infantry Division, Bravo Company, 1st Platoon, 1st Squad.

Home was a small firebase called Pershing, located about forty to fifty miles west of Saigon near the Cambodian border. Since arriving in Nam a little less than a month before, this country boy had been in the field as a grunt, going into rice paddies and jungles to set up night ambushes. Success had been limited. My platoon had surprised and blown away several Viet Cong coming from and going to local villages in our area. Most of the night ambushes were set up using a squad of eight to ten men. If VC were known to be in an area, the entire platoon would set up an ambush to ensure greater firepower.

During the day, the platoon would go to a holding area in the jungle or in rice paddies, or even in a local village. The guys would lie around, sleep, or write letters, anything to pass away the hours.

About an hour or two before sunset the platoon would get ready to move out. On the night of January 5th, 1970, my platoon joined the rest of the company to set up a Master Ambush. Just before dark, the company arrived at a huge field covered with knee-high grass. You could see hedgerows along both sides. To the south, the field gave way to the jungle; to the north there was a large clump of trees, and a village beyond them.

Robert M. Braun, Sr.

The company commander advised my lieutenant that the company would spread out across the field in squads. We had three platoons (six squads) in our company, a total of about 60 men. Each unit would be spread out across this huge field at about 20 to 30 yards apart, like railroad ties on a train track. My squad was the second to get into position. As I watched the rest of the company file past, I wondered what the hell we were doing. During the short time I had been in Nam, I had never set up an ambush without some kind of cover.

Instinct warned me that there could be trouble. The silhouettes of the men from the squads on either side of me were barely visible as I dug a shallow foxhole to provide some type of protection. While watching the last of the sunlight fade away, this inexperienced country boy couldn't help but wonder what would happen if Viet Cong appeared between the squads. If my squad or one of the others had to open fire, there was a good chance that some of our own men would be injured or even killed by friendly fire. No one could understand why we had set up that way, since we could not open fire on any VC without shooting at each other.

Nonetheless, I was powerless to alter my situation. I had been programmed to listen to my superiors, right or wrong. The only thing I could do was to pray that we did not see anything. The night started as a carbon copy of any other night I had been on ambush patrol: two men taking an hour shift on watch while the others slept. Sleep came easily that night because the heat of the day and the long march had drained me.

Soon I was quietly awakened by Jack, the man next to me. He informed me that we had received a call over the radio that the 1st Squad of the 3rd Platoon had spotted gooks. Knowing that the 1st Squad of the 3rd Platoon was directly in front of me, no more than 60 to 70 yards away, I pressed myself deeper into my shallow foxhole, waiting for the action to start.

I feared that one of us would be killed or hurt by the burst of rifle and machine-gun fire that was expected at any time. None of us wanted to be shot and certainly not by our own men. We waited for what seemed like a lifetime for the action to begin, but there was nothing except the stillness of the night. What was wrong? Why weren't the VC blown away?

Normally, the VC traveled in small groups, and Standard Operating Procedure (SOP) was to allow the first few of them to

73

pass by until their main force was in front of our main force. Then we would blow them away. Following this plan, the 1st Squad of the 3rd Platoon started to count the gooks as they passed by. Lieutenant Sparks received muffled radio calls that the first count was five, then ten, then twenty and still counting. By this time, we all were hoping that our ambush would not be revealed.

I strained to spot the VC from my position, but it was a moonless night, and the gooks were too far away for me to see. I was scared. Sweat poured off me, as I wondered whether or not I would see the light of the next sunrise.

As the minutes dragged on, the count continued to rise to more than fifty. Also, it was reported that these were not the local black pajama VC we were accustomed to fighting. They were the well-armed NVA's (North Vietnam Army), reportedly carrying AK-47s, mortars, recoilless rifles, and heavy machine-guns. They were walking single file about five to seven feet apart.

I sank even lower into my totally inadequate foxhole, wishing that I had more time to dig it deeper, afraid that I would end up in hand-to-hand combat with a force that was most likely more seasoned and better armed than my own. Was I going to survive the night? Was I ever, going home?

Finally, after what seemed to be the longest ten minutes of my life, the count stopped at seventy-two. We all laid motionless for a long time after the NVA's had passed, afraid we might still be discovered.

Air strikes and artillery were called in to where the NVA's were thought to have headed. We watched the bombs explode, sending smoke and flames high into the sky, hoping the light would not reveal our position.

After the bombing, my squad was split in two, so that half the men could be on watch while the other half slept: a half hour on, a half hour off. I was too excited and nervous to sleep. Just the thought of being that close to a large well-armed force sent shivers up and down my spine.

As the night passed, I continued to gaze through my squad's starlight scope and into the darkness, hoping that nothing would appear, counting the minutes to sunrise and the safety of the light. I was afraid that, in the dark, the enemy would walk right over us. The image of a long line of NVA's, appearing out of the blackness and coming right toward us, haunted me.

After a few hours, the squad hoped that the danger had passed. However, around 0130 hours, my ghostly vision almost came true. The lieutenant received a call over the radio that the 1st squad of the 2nd platoon, about 50 yards from where I was, had spotted gooks coming from where the NVA's had been going earlier.

As the count continued, we all realized that it was the same force of NVA's and that the bombs had missed their target. Perhaps the only thing it did was alert the NVA's that we were in the area.

Again, the fear of being spotted was in everyone's minds. We all knew that because of the way our company was situated, we didn't stand a chance if we had to engage a force of this size in combat. Our only hope was to remain silent and hope the darkness would conceal our position.

Everyone was afraid to move as the count continued. Finally, the last of the NVAs passed through the company. Again, everyone stayed still a long time as the last of the NVAs passed.

The sun finally started to rise, changing the uncertainty of darkness to the security of light. The whole squad was facing east, looking toward the rising sun, feeling lucky to have survived the night. It was a beautiful sunrise. The oranges and yellows played off the few clouds that were in the sky. The air around us was beginning to feel warm. You could tell that it was going to be another hot day, but no one seemed to care.

Even today, I love to see the sun rising. I think how important every minute of life is. Most people don't know or appreciate what they have. Maybe they would if they had to live through the hours and minutes wondering if they were going to survive a night.

This was one of the most unbelievable nights I spent in Vietnam. Not a single shot was fired, but it was one of the longest and scariest nights during my tour of duty. All of us were innocent young men just trying to get home. I am not afraid to admit I was terrified the entire time I was there, from my first step out of the plane until the time they wheeled me onto the Medevac plane to leave.

Robert M. Braun, Sr.

First Purple Heart

It was January 25th, 1970, I was finally able to finish writing my letter home that I started on the 20th. I had been in Vietnam for a little over a month. My platoon was just back from a week in the bush and had the day off to rest.

Later in the day on January 20th my squad received orders that we would be on duty the next day to fly into an area where possible VC were spotted, called a Hot Landing Zone or Hot LZ.

On January 21st, 1970, around 0730 hours we got word that some VC were reported, and three helicopters were going to fly us out. We all moved out to the landing pads ready to fly out when the choppers arrived.

It was already heating up; sweat was beading up; it was going to be another hot day. We were all dressed in jungle fatigues, fully armed with hand grenades and ammo. A number of men in the squad had M-16 rifles. One man, we called Brownie, carried a M-60 machine-gun, and I was armed with a M-79 grenade launcher. We did not pack our normal load of food and just enough water for this mission since our squad was expected to be back later that day. Ref. 10

My squad had been on a Hot LZ mission a few times, every assignment was different so; we did not know what to expect. My squad had been lucky so far, we hadn't been confronted with our enemy on any Hot LZ or our night ambushes.

Soon three choppers flew in kicking up dust. As soon as the three helicopters landed, we climbed in. It didn't take long to where some VC were spotted. We landed in a small field with a hedgerow to our left. I had my M-79 loaded with a high explosive fragmentation round ready to fire if given the order. Ref. 11

On an earlier mission that my unit had completed, and while waiting for the choppers to arrive to take us back to FSB Pershing: two of the other guys that carried the M-79, and I, had the opportunity to practice using it. The other guys ran out of the high explosive rounds; I had so many, I was able to give them some of mine.

I learned in Basic Training that to become an expert shot you had to practice. The incentive for me was, if you received an expert in training, you would receive a weekend pass. Since I only lived about twenty miles from my Basic Training Base, Fort Dix, New Jersey, a weekend pass meant, I was going home.

A couple of days before we were going to be tested with the M-14, the rifle I used during Basic Training, my entire Basic Training Company went to the rifle range to practice. During the practice each trainee shot one hundred eighty-six rounds at targets. The flop down targets were arranged at different distances. You would receive a hit when the target flipped backwardly. Ref. 12

I wasn't happy with my first round because I would not have received an expert and wouldn't have received a weekend pass. I asked the sergeant if I could have another round, and did a lot better the second round. For the next few days, I had a painful bruised right shoulder.

It was worth it, since the next week at the rifle test I ended up second best in the company and earned a weekend pass, another weekend home with my family and friends.

Once out of the choppers we lined up to search the area. As we moved toward the hedgerow, we spotted what looked like a tunnel. My friend Jack was told to throw a hand grenade into the tunnel. After Jack threw the hand grenade he ran back to where I was kneeling, his back to the hedgerow. As soon as the grenade went off, I felt an impact to my left shoulder and neck.

Feeling no pain and after checking for blood, and since I didn't see any, I didn't realize that I had been hit. I went over to Jack who had been hit by a piece of shrapnel in his back side, to see if he was alright. As I was walking Jack to our medic, I saw blood running down my left arm. A piece of shrapnel had hit and entered my arm and luckily, a piece had bounced off my collar bone.

Jack and I were dusted off about twenty minutes later and flown to Cu Chi, the Twenty-Fifth's Division Headquarters to the 12th Evacuation Hospital. I had a slight cut on my neck and a piece of shrapnel in my left shoulder. X-rays were taken which showed the shrapnel in my shoulder was too deep to be

12th Evacuation Hospital
Landing Pad

taken out and no shrapnel in my neck. I was given four stitches in my left shoulder, and a bandage on my neck.

The physician who put the stitches in told me I was fortunate. Had I been hit one half inch upwardly and to the right in my neck, the shrapnel would have severed either my carotid or jugular artery, and I would have died within minutes. Ref. 13

Later, Jack and I found out that our two-point men had been injured by a booby trap. Both were injured badly. One lost his right leg below the knee and severely injured his left leg. His days in Vietnam were over. The other point man, who we called Pusher, received shrapnel to his left side and eventually returned to our unit out in the field.

Jack's shrapnel in his back side was in too deep to be taken out. He received a few stitches and had trouble sitting the next few days. We had to stay in Cu Chi for five to six days so our wounds could be evaluated and treated.

After we were cared for, we walked to our company's headquarters in Cu Chi where we would be staying for the next few days: out of the action, away from the fighting, and a little closer to the end of our tour.

Jack and I were lucky because, it was the practice that when a guy became a short-timer (not much time left on his one-year tour) they would be removed from the field and be assigned to a safer position. A guy that was just out in the field and was a member of our squad was assigned to an Officers Mess Hall.

The next few nights, Jack and I had a number of feasts. We hadn't had any home cooking in a while, mostly C-rations when out in the fields and some mess hall meals when back in FSB Pershing.

I can tell you one thing and that is, the officers in Cu Chi eat a lot better than those of us in the field. We had roast chicken with baked potatoes, steaks, salads with fresh greens, tomatoes, and freshly made apple pie. We washed it all down with some really good wine; then had a few beers.

They were great nights. We were out of the field, in a safe place, and had some great meals. It might have been worth getting hit. I was lucky, they weren't bad injuries but, I will be carrying the shrapnel in my left shoulder for the rest of my life.

Cu Chi Steam Bath

Robert M. Braun, Sr.

Making the most of our time in Cu Chi, a few days later, we visited the steam bath, where we each received a massage from pretty young Vietnamese girls. The girl massaging me kept picking up the white hand towel covering my manhood and talking Vietnamese to the girl massaging Jack. It was a great time; you could almost forget you were in a War Zone.

One night we were sitting around having a few beers and we talked again, about "The Bob Hope Christmas Show". Jack was in the field, so he did not have the opportunity to see it.

He was shocked that I not only saw it but guarded the stage the night before the show. I told him "The Bob Hope Christmas Show" was in an area called the Lightning Bowl. Neil Armstrong, Les Brown and His Band of Renown, Suzanne Charny, The Golddiggers, Teresa Graves, Miss World 1968, Penelope Plummer, of Australia, Linda Bennett, Kelly Hope, Rosie Grier, and Connie Stevens, along with Bob Hope, were in the show.

I told Jack one of Bob Hope's jokes that received one of the biggest laughs was: *"it's nice to be here at Cu Chi by the Sea ... VC, that is."*

When Connie Stevens was going to sing the song "Bill" she asked the crowd if there was anyone out there named Bill. Instantly, a large number of men raised their hands. Connie picked one guy to come up on the stage and she sang "Bill" to the guy.

After the song the guy admitted his name wasn't Bill which got a huge reaction from the crowd. When it finally settled down, Connie sang "16 Reasons Why I Love You". You could have heard a pin drop. It got so quiet.

When I was sitting at the show the song brought back some good and bad memories. When I was a sophomore in high school, I started going out with a freshman who was a doctor's daughter. She loved to sing and dance to the song and sang it to me often.

I knew she was out of my league being a doctor's daughter, one of the smartest in her freshman class, and was the number one seat in the flute section, but she was my first love.

I ended up losing her to a senior when they were in the play "West Side Story". The song reminded me of my broken heart, my life at home, and my family back in the states.

79

After five days we were given the OK to rejoin our unit and joined the daily convoy back to FSB Pershing. It was a long ride of about twenty-three miles on a dusty dirt road with all kinds of traffic from oxen carts to tanks. It was good to see the sign "Welcome to Fire Support Base Pershing, the home of the White Warriors", after the long dirty ride.

The day after we joined our unit, we were assigned a mission and Jack was well enough to join. Because my injuries were not healed enough, I spent the next five days in FSB Pershing. It was probably the most boring five days I spent in Vietnam.

It did give me time to write home and tell them about my injuries and my last few missions. It also gave me time to think about walking point.

When Jack and I were told our squad's point men were injured, Jack and I talked about volunteering to walk point. We knew that the life expectancy for point men in Vietnam was between a few weeks and twenty seconds, dependent upon how active the area being patrolled. The area we patrolled was very active. We knew that the point position was dangerous but, it was really important to have a couple of guys that could be trusted leading. You can see from the map the Ho Chi Minh Trail ends right where Jack and I were stationed and would be walking point.

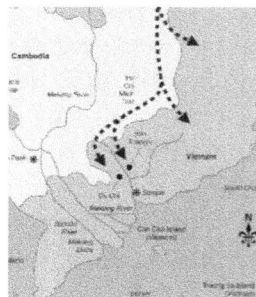

We both had a lot of experience in the woods and quickly became trusted by the other men in our platoon. Eventually, we did volunteer to walk point and ended up walking it for a little over two months.

Now, I will continue describing the missions that I wrote about in a letter to my home, that I had started writing on the 20th.

On the twelfth we were flown out to an area just outside of Cu Chi. It surprised us we found a tunnel complex. While a couple of guys in my platoon were searching a tunnel, I saw a trail going into some thick bush. I went up the trail and found a lot of dead fish and a larger tunnel system and a few booby traps were found. No contact was made with the VC even though they were in the area just before we got there. The tunnel rats were flown in and a number of mortars were found in the tunnels that were believed to be used to fire into Cu Chi, along with maps and other documents.

On Friday, the fourteenth, we were flown to an area I believe that was near the Saigon River. The choppers couldn't land so we had to jump out from about six feet into a rice paddy. The water and mud were up to our knees. We made it to a dike where it was dry and out of the water. After walking on the dikes for a while we came to a place where we had to get off the dike to cross a rice paddy. The water was up to my waist. It was so hot it was good being in the water, we just had to make sure our weapons didn't get wet.

Later, when on a break, near a stream, I heard some noise in the stream behind me. I got up to check out the noise and found an old man in a small sampan loaded with rice. I pulled him over and after we checked his boat, we let the old man go.

Writing home about my last few missions, I assured my Mother and family that I don't take chances, almost always have someone with me, and that the wounds I received weren't serious. Jack and I would be receiving Purple Hearts for our injuries and would send them home when we received them.

In the letter, I told my family, a little about my friend Jack, that he had become my best friend, and that he was a lot like Rich, my twin. I got to know a lot about Jack during the time we were together recovering from our wounds.

Jack was from the small town of Clarion, Iowa, the largest producer of eggs in the world. His father worked for the Iowa Highway Commission as the foreman for his area. His mother worked as a cashier at a local grocery store that was owned by

Wright County Courthouse and Clock Tower

one of Jack's best friends, Scott Case's parents. Jack and Scott were both bag boys at the same grocery store. Both his father and mother sometimes worked part time in a local tavern owned by one of his father's friends. Ref. 14

I knew that Jack was a good athlete; he had already told me he was the quarterback and co-captain for his high school football and basketball teams, that he played shortstop for baseball, was one of the starting guards for his basketball team, and was on the track and golf teams.

He told me about the great game he and his good friend Scott Case had at the Hampton Homecoming where his football team won 32 to 19; that he ran a fourth quarter kickoff for a 58-yard touchdown, and hit his teammate Jerry Boyington for an 83-yard pass for another touchdown. The person who was the happiest, after his parents, was his football and baseball coach,

Jack running the football, from his high school yearbook.

Wayne Bergstrom. He said that Coach Bergstrom was a big influence in his life, that he had him as a middle school teacher in Math and Social Studies. I learned more about Coach Bergstrom over the next few months we were together. I was impressed, knew Jack had heart, and was a great teammate, a lot like my twin brother.

After he graduated from high school, he played football at Wartburg College for one year then withdrew at the start of his sophomore year. Jack never told me why he withdrew, then he was drafted. He did tell me he majored in Liberal Arts, and got OK grades.

I told him I was one of the starting forwards for my high school basketball team, and that I had a great game helping my team beat the sixth ranked team in the state of New Jersey in a Christmas Tournament. My basketball team had a great year! We ended up tying for the league championship and won a couple of state tournament games. We scored over a hundred points in four games, the only team in our high school history to score a hundred points or more, and there was no three-point line nor any dunking.

Jack also knew my older brother was drafted by the Minnesota Twins in 1967 in the eleventh round and that he had played two years of ball in the Twins Gulf Coast Rookie Affiliates in Sarasota, Florida before he was drafted into the Army. He was lucky enough to be stationed in Germany where he was able to play baseball and was named the All-Star shortstop for the All-Europe Championship Baseball Team. He was getting out of the Army in September while I was just starting my time with the Army. One of our friends had a coming home party for my older brother and a going away party for me.

I told Jack about how my parents, my twin, and I drove to Florida for two weeks of my brother's first year and was able to retrieve the baseball from his first homerun. My twin, a friend, and I drove to Sarasota for my brother's second year and I told Jack how much more fun we had without our parents.

We also talked about playing football in our early years. He told me he played football growing up in all the youth football programs.

I told him that I played midget football growing up, coached by my father but, not throughout school because my high school didn't have a football team.

I did tell him about playing the All-Stars from Fort Dix, New Jersey, where I ended up doing my Basic Training. It was the start of the second half and I was the end on the right side. The running back for the All-Star team came my way and I made a real good tackle, but saw stars. After the tackle, the running back looked at me and said, "Nice tackle". The running back ended up being a guy named Franco Harris who was the running back for Penn State University, played thirteen years for the NFL, and was inducted into the Pro Football Hall of Fame in 1990. Ref. 15

While we were at Cu Chi and staying at our company's headquarters, we got a chance to play a little basketball. Our headquarters had a small court with a ten-foot basket. We couldn't do much to start because of our injuries, but it was almost like home.

Growing up my twin and I spent hours playing on the court in our backyard. Our court was dirt, much like the one at our company's headquarters. After a few days we had healed enough to shoot baskets. I showed Jack my twin's and my practice shooting routine.

It went like this; if the shooter makes his first shot the shooter continues to shoot until he misses: then continues shooting until he makes a shot, then continues until he misses again. This encouraged the shooter to make the first shot. The rebounder would practice tapping the ball in or go high for a rebound. A couple of times I jumped high enough with two hands to just lay the miss into the basket. Jack liked the practice routine and was impressed with my jumping ability. I told him that my brothers and I did jumps every night; first to the doorway and then to the ceiling. Our Mother always complained about handprints on the ceiling. He said he wished he had a brother with whom he could have practiced.

I was lucky, to not only have a brother, but I also had an identical twin with whom I could practice. I had shown him the watch I got from my twin for Christmas; how every time I looked at it, I thought about my twin and family. We ended up talking a lot about our families. He was surprised that I was from a family of nine kids, four boys and five girls. He was also surprised when I refused orders from our Captain.

We were walking just outside a village and there was a group of women and children with a few water buffaloes walking on a dirt road. The captain wanted me to use my M-79 to shoot a high explosive round close, to scare them. I refused by saying "No Sir". He ordered me again and I responded with, "No Sir, I don't want to hurt them. I have only fired the M-79 a few times and am not sure of its range." He responded with, "OK, I understand". It was one of the reasons a few of us were able to practice with the M-79 on a previous mission.

Jack said he couldn't believe I refused the Captain and said he would have refused also. He said, a bunch of other guys in our squad would have refused as well. It's maybe one of the reasons I was being treated a little differently.

Jack and I had a good time shooting shots and hanging around for the next five days. We would listen to the radio while having a few beers each night and went to the NCO club. One of Jack's songs he wanted to hear was by Johnny Rivers, "Poor Side of Town". Now, every time I listen to this song, I feel Jack's broken heart.

After a few beers, we joined in on the singing of the songs: especially the song "We Got to Get out of this Place" by the Animals.

Another song, by Creedence Clearwater Revival I liked was "Susie Q". It was my twin's favorite song because, he was engaged to a girl named Sue.

We liked the Beatles, Beach Boys, Diana Ross and The Supremes, and many other bands. Jack also told me about his friend named Scott Case, who he first met at age four. They were best friends and both played on their high school's football and baseball teams.

Scott was an All-State singer, with Pam Burt, Jack's high school sweetheart, and Scott bleached his hair blond to sing with a local rock band called the "Exiles". Jack said he would tag along to the gigs and hang out with the band. These were great nights; it was almost like we were back in the states.

One night when we were listening to the radio, I asked him to tell me the story again, how he and one of his best friends, Tom Blecker, saved a volunteer firefighter. Jack said, they were sitting in Tom's 1959 Chevy listening to Johnny Rivers "Poor Side of Town". There was an explosion, and a fire engulfed a warehouse. They heard a voice cry for help. They saved a fireman whose hands were burned to the bone. The story was in the local papers honoring them as heroes.

I told Jack how one night after a party, a friend and I were on our way to an all-night diner to have some breakfast. As we went around a bend, on a dark country road, on the side of the road there was a car turned over on the driver's side. Inside was a man that was dazed. My friend stopped and we both tried to pull the driver's side door open. It wouldn't budge. I told my friend to watch out, and I pulled the door right off its hinges and threw the door aside, like it was as light as a feather, allowing the driver to crawl out of the overturned car. We left before the police arrived after making sure the driver was ok.

Jack wasn't my twin, but was a damn good replacement. Over the next few months, we would grow even closer.

I really couldn't complain about being out of the field for a few days, since I was mostly out of harm's way, and I'd been in country for thirty-nine days with only three hundred and twenty-six days left on my tour. I was

Mess hall at FSB Pershing

able to get some hot meals at the mess hall in FSB Pershing. It wasn't Mother's cooking but at least it was hot.

When the rest of the squad got back from their mission, we received orders that we were being moved to a new firebase called FSB Kien further west and closer towards the Cambodian/Vietnam border. The rear headquarters moved from Cu Chi Base Camp to Dau Tieng.

This is the certificate that I sent home for my first Purple heart.

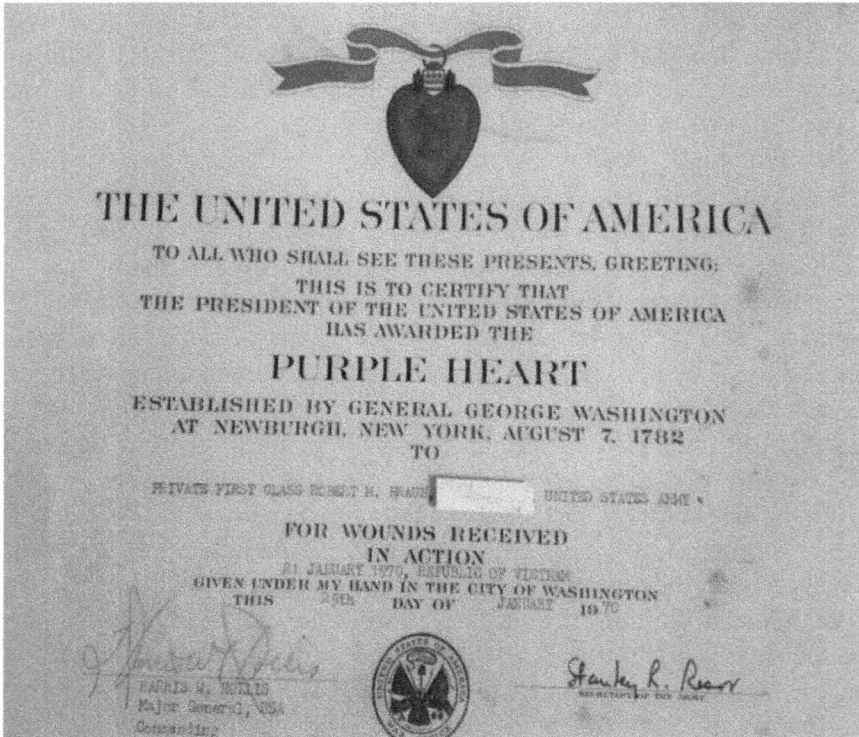

The Purple Heart was given in the name of the President and is awarded to any U. S. Armed Services member who was wounded or killed in any action fighting an enemy of the United States.

It is the oldest military award given to a U. S. military member. It was originally designed as the Badge of Military Merit and was established by George Washington in 1782. It was only awarded to soldiers of the Revolutionary War by General Washington.

The Purple Heart was first awarded on February 22, 1932 and is now eligible to all military personnel.

Approximately 430,000 have been given to individuals killed in action and has been received by over 2,000,000 recipients.

Robert M. Braun, Sr.

My Twenty-first Birthday

I had been in Vietnam for fifty-five days stationed with the 2nd battalion, 12th Infantry, 25th Infantry Division, Bravo Company, 1st Platoon, 1st Squad. We had just moved to a new firebase called FSB Kien. It was located further north, closer to the Cambodian border and in War Zone C.

It was a couple days before my twenty-first birthday. I was writing home to tell my family about my last few missions. I had some time to write because we had the day off with just guard duty at night after a short assignment. I wrote that I couldn't believe Dickaloo, my twin and I were going to be twenty-one. The next day, a day before my/our birthday, we were being flown out to the field again.

I had to tease Rich because I was going to turn twenty-one thirteen hours before him. I asked him how it felt being the youngest twin. He was born ten minutes before me and never let me forget it. How I missed my family and my twin.

I couldn't finish this letter because I had to get ready to go out into the jungle to hunt for Charlie. The next day we were picked up to check out a village that the VC and NVA visited at night. It was going to be a hairy mission.

On the 8th of February, the day before our birthday, my platoon was on the chopper pad to be flown out to check the village. When the choppers arrived, we all climbed in. It didn't take long to reach our drop-off point. We were set down in a field near the village.

After being dropped off we moved in to check out the village that had a number of homes, most were made of what looked like bundles of straw. All of the buildings had dirt floors with no glass windows but wooden doors to close in case of rain. We moved around the village checking each building.

In a few buildings, mothers and young children sat quietly with a fearful look. One mother was feeding her baby rice from a bowl. The bowl of rice had ants crawling all over it and a number of ants were crawling on the baby's face. Seeing this, made me realize how lucky I was, and how good I really had it back home in New Jersey.

After we searched the village, we went to a holding area to wait out the day. It was another hot day much like the day before and the next. We found a shady place and waited until dusk to move out to where the night ambush would be. Around 1930 hours we moved out to our ambush site but were told not to get too comfortable because, we would be moving out around 2300 hours, an hour before my birthday. At 2300 hours, we moved out to join the rest of the platoon, then the whole company, then two other companies, to surround the village.

As we were moving around the village, the lead company ran into some VC trying to leave the village. Bullets began to fly overhead; we all had to hit the ground. I began to wonder if I was going to see my twenty-first birthday. The lead company ended up killing three VC and it is unknown how many got away. There were firefights all night, but my squad was lucky, we were not involved in any of them.

The whole day I continued to think about home and what my twin would be doing, going to a local bar to have a few, now that he could drink legally.

Growing up we did our share of drinking. Riding around on the backroads on weekends and/or going to a party, we would have a few. We were lucky. One summer while working for the Washington Crossing State Park in New Jersey, I was sent to the Princeton Battlefield to mow the fields where the battle of Princeton occurred during the Revolutionary War on January 3rd, 1777.

Monument at the Princeton Battlefield Park

It was a hot day so I stopped by the monument at the battlefield to take a break. To my surprise I found a wallet with an ID for someone who had just turned twenty-one that looked a lot like my twin and me; about six-foot tall, light brown hair, blue eyes, and weighed one-hundred seventy pounds. We were able to use the ID to purchase alcohol. Since we were already eighteen, no one questioned it.

The Princeton Battlefield is a six hundred eighty-one-acre park that is where the Battle of Princeton occurred and where General Mercer lost his life. Ref. 16

Some say it was the bloodiest battle of the Revolutionary War; where Washington rallied the American soldiers to push back a British assault to cap ten days of fighting that included three battles that began when Washington and his men crossed the Delaware River on that cold winter night on December 25th, 1776.

It was a place I enjoyed going and cutting the acres of grass, plus sometimes there were some pretty girls visiting the park. There was a Meeting

The Meeting House in Princeton, NJ

House near the park that was built in 1735. The present Meeting House was built in 1765 after a fire destroyed the original Meeting House. The Meeting House was used to treat both the Americans and British soldiers injured during the battle. Even today you will find blood stains on the wooden floorboards. Ref. 17

Not too far from the park is the location of the Institute for Advanced Studies, where Albert Einstein studied and walked. Sometimes I would walk to the Institute during lunch break just to be where Albert Einstein had been, and maybe walk where he may have walked. Ref. 18

So, I knew my twin would be having a few in a bar that is on the corner of where the Washington Crossing Bridge crosses the Delaware River, while I was in a battle in Vietnam, wondering whether I was going to survive the night.

At 0600 hours on the day of the ninth, the birthday of my twin and I, my unit was picked up and flown to Cu Chi for a Stand Down.

I knew Jack was a pretty good basketball player; he had told me he was one of the starting guards for his high school basketball team. When we were in Cu Chi recovering from our first shrapnel injuries, we played a little one on one, along with our shooting practice routine. We didn't keep score but it was close. This is how we played; if you make a shot you keep the ball, misses you go for the rebound, you get it, you keep the ball, like a real game. Jack stole the ball from me a few times and then made some easy baskets. I blamed it on the dirt court, he claimed it was his speed. We had a real good time and a lot of laughs.

Jack was a little different than playing with my twin. My twin and I would end up fighting when we played against each other. He was very competitive and didn't like to lose, so we always played as a team and we didn't lose, very often. Jack and I didn't fight. When I made a good move or shot, he would compliment me and I did the same to him. We really became a team and it showed when we played other units when on the Stand Down.

During the Vietnam War a Stand Down was a time away from the battlefield when soldiers could rest from combat and take care of personal hygiene, eat warm meals, drink a few beers, receive medical and dental care, and enjoy the camaraderie of battle buddies in a safe environment. Ref. 19

There was a full court asphalt basketball court and we split up in five-man teams; Jack, Brownie, Lopez, a tall new member of our squad, and I, made up our team. The rule was, whichever team scored ten baskets, each basket was only one point, was the winner and the winning team continued to play.

These were the members of my basketball team.

Jack and I played together like we had been doing it forever, like how my twin and I played. Our team didn't lose a game. We all played together as a team just like we did when out in the field.

It was really hot and we were soaking wet from sweat, but we didn't care, we had almost gotten used to the heat. During breaks in the games, and when we ate, or when a couple other teams played, we had a few beers. It was my twenty-first birthday, so in celebration they saluted me and we had a couple birthday beers.

This reminded me of home, without the beers. Throughout the year, we would play basketball games with kids in the neighborhood. We had a tall thin tree that we used as a long pole with lights on top, so we could play games or practice at night.

During the Stand Down a ceremony was held to give Jack and me our first Purple Hearts. We both were able to send them home.

It was hard leaving our Stand Down after having a few days out of the field and celebrating my twenty-first birthday.

This is not the actual ceremony at Cu Chi for Jack and me, but one similar to it.

When we got back to FSB Kien it was the Eleventh of February and it was Ash Wednesday. Jack, me, and some other members of our platoon attended Mass to receive our ashes. It was the start of Lent but being in a war zone we ate whatever and whenever we could. Out in the field we ate C-rations and had two hot meals when back in the firebase.

The next day we attended a service that was for the death of a fellow infantry man from Charlie Company that was killed in the previous week. This was another time the magnitude of the war really hit me, knowing that every time I leave the somewhat safe and secure firebase, my life was in danger. I ended up going to several of these services. None of them were very easy to attend, and all reminded me to be vigilant.

Robert M. Braun, Sr.

This is my second article that was published in a national magazine in the late 1990s. There have been additions to the original article.

Top of the World, Ma!

It was the middle of February, 1970 and I'd been in the country for over two months. My tour was getting shorter, only a little over 300 days to go. The companies of the 2nd and 12th, 25th Infantry had just taken over the area we were now patrolling from the 1st Infantry Division, better known as the Big Red One. I was with the Bravo Company, 1st Platoon, 1st Squad. We had been trucked up from FSB Pershing to FSB Kien, glimpsing Tay Ninh in the distance as we traveled west towards the Cambodian Vietnam border.

We had not gotten used to the new terrain, a thick hot insect and snake infested jungle, and our squad was now going out on patrols for five to ten days at a stretch, marching through the endless hot jungle looking for Viet Cong.

I had volunteered to walk point with my best friend Jack Rae Smith and we had been walking it for a little less than a month. It was a position that brought us closer to the action and placed the burden of survival on our shoulders. We didn't have to depend on someone else who might walk us into an ambush. Walking point in the area around FSB Pershing was easy most of the time, the land was flat with only patches of jungle and hedgerows. Many times, we were flown into an area to check hot spots, or were out only four days to a week on night ambushes. We could travel along the dikes of the rice paddies, relatively confident that the dikes would not be booby trapped.

We got back from one week on patrol, to be informed that our platoon would be flown the next day to a 1,000-foot mountain, we called it Pine Ridge, the Vietnamese called it Black Virgin Mountain, for a two-week stay. The area around the mountain was very active as the Ho Ch Minh Trail ended a few kilometers west across the Cambodian border.

Robert M. Braun, Sr.

Variations of the legend of Núi Bà Đen or Black Virgin Mountain exist. The oldest Khmer myth involves a female deity, "Neang Khmau" who left her footprints on the mountain rocks. The Vietnamese myth centers around a woman, Bà Đen, falling in love with a soldier and then through betrayal or suicide Bà Đen dies on the mountain. Ref. 19

The firebase on the mountain was used to fire rounds into the jungle below. It seemed like a hell of a lot easier assignment than tramping around the insect infested and dangerous jungle in 100-plus degree heat carrying seventy to one-hundred pounds of ammo, food, and water.

At 0600 hours we were fully armed on the LZ (landing zone), waiting to be flown to the mountain. Soon, a twin blade Chinook helicopter came roaring in to transport us. It was my first time on the big chopper. The noise was deafening as it approached the LZ. It hung in the air as it neared the ground, its wheels touched down as the engines slowed.

Once inside, we all sat while the big chopper lifted off. It took a few seconds for my eyes to adjust to the darkness of the belly of the big helicopter. When it took off, it banked left, causing my stomach to rise up to my throat, as if I were on one of the thrill rides, I rode as a kid.

It did not take long for us to reach the mountain. The sun was low in the cloudless sky, casting long shadows pointing west. Darkness hung onto the tops of the jungles below and I could feel the coolness and the dryness of the air. I felt as if I were going to some safe Shangri-La or on R&R.

R&R, or 'rest and recreation', gave soldiers serving in Vietnam a brief respite from the war. United States servicemen on a twelve-month tour of duty were given seven days R&R outside Vietnam. In the early part of the war, they could spend this time in one of several Asian cities or Hawaii. Hawaii was the most visited place for R&R. Ref. 20

Because I knew about the R&R I was hoping to use it to get back to the States for my twin's wedding.

At least for the next two weeks the heat would not be sapping and draining my energy. Right away, I felt away from the fighting, somewhat safe: confident that I was two weeks closer to home.

After landing, we moved into the small firebase composed of four 105-millimeter howitzers, mortar pits, and some weather worn buildings. One of the buildings was used as headquarters and storage, while another was used as a small mess hall and kitchen. Around the firebase ran bunkers, and then row after row of barbed wire. Further out on the south and north sides were lookout posts. Other than the landing zone and the buildings, there were very few areas that were flat.

Large rocks laid everywhere; we had to walk around them to get from one side of the base to the other. The tree line was well below the rows of barbed wire. You could see for miles.

The platoon's responsibility was to guard and protect the artillery men. Jack, my best buddy, and I agreed to volunteer to take the lookout post that faced north. Since we had been walking together at point, we were used to being out on our own.

Carrying a radio, some supplies, our weapons, and ammo, we weaved our way to the bunker that would be our home for the next two weeks. The bunker was well fortified; sandbags surrounded four walls of ammo boxes filled with sand and dirt. On top of the bunker there was a 50-caliber machine-gun. Ref. 21

The only time I'd seen a 50-caliber machine-gun in action was when we were flying into a hot LZ, the door gunner ripping apart the jungle, shooting at the unseen Viet Cong. I was impressed watching its six-inch casings flying everywhere and flames shooting out the end of the barrel. I'd envied the firepower and wished that I could carry one while on patrol.

I remember how tranquil and beautiful it was, looking at the jungle below. It was like looking at a huge dark green field of tightly grown broccoli heads. On a clear day, I felt I could almost see home. It was hard to believe that the jungle below harbored so many dangers and death itself.

The big guns boomed both day and night. Sometimes I could see the flash of the bombs they shot out crashing into the forest below. At night I would often see the red tracers of rifles, reminding me that my fellow grunts were engaging in action. Knowing the Viet Cong were out there somewhere, kept us alert.

One night, while on watch, I was looking out into the blackness when suddenly, one of the trip flares burst into life, momentarily blinding me with its brilliant light. Something must have tripped it. Shivers shot down my spine thinking that we were being attacked. I quickly reported it and was instructed to open up with the 50-caliber machine-gun.

It roared into action sending out green tracers. Flames reached out into the night. As the gun spit out the empty brass casings of the large shells, I aimed at the ground around the flare and sprayed the area in front of me, watching the rocks and dirt fly. If I wasn't so frightened, it would have been fun.

I was afraid that we were being overrun and would have to fight hand-to-hand combat. Unexpectedly, this peaceful two-week assignment had the potential of turning into a nightmare.

Jack rushed up to the top of the bunker and was firing his M-16. The cool dry air was filled with smoke that smelled of sulfur. We continued to lay down a hail of bullets as the flare burned, then we stopped firing to listen to the sounds of the night. The only thing we could hear was the flare spending itself; it went out as suddenly as it had burst into life.

We were ordered to go on a one-hundred percent watch. As the night dragged slowly by, Jack and I peered into the darkness. The only light was from the tiny specks of stars that filled the sky. This was the kind of night we most hated, the type of night on which the VC liked to attack.

Neither of us had to tell the other how worried we were; we had grown so close that we worked as one. We knew we were too far from the rest of the platoon for help, so we had to protect each other. Jack had my back, and I had his. For the rest of the night, we took turns sitting behind the 50-caliber machine-gun, ready to fire. Finally, the eastern sky began to lighten, the grays turning to blues and finally yellows and oranges, another great sunrise. We were another day closer to the world and another day shorter.

Robert M. Braun, Sr.

The days and nights dragged by. During the day it was so hot we could walk around in shorts and no shirt. We were working on a seashore-type tan. But at night it got so cold that we had to wear a flight jacket and were still cold. The only things to do were to listen to the radio, sleep, write home, read old letters or paperback books, and talk about growing up.

It was a special treat to receive a letter and especially a package. A chopper would arrive almost every day to bring in supplies, ammo, and mail. Jack and I would take turns each day to weave around the boulders to the mess hall to get our meals, mail, talk to some of the other guys in our unit, or anything else we needed.

One day I got a couple letters, one from my Mother and one from a high school ex-girlfriend. My Mother's letter informed me that my older brother received another contract with the Minnesota Twins and a raise. I was really happy for my brother and bragged to Jack that my brother would be playing in the Major Leagues in two years. My older brother did make it to the Majors in two years and played Major League Baseball for fifteen years, winning the World Series in 1982 with the St. Louis Cardinals.

My Mother also informed me that the younger kids were getting used to their new schools. They had sold the house where I grew up, and were living temporarily in Trenton, New Jersey, at my grandmother's home that my Mother had inherited; until their new house was built in Titusville near our old home in Washington Crossing, New Jersey.

Jack already knew I grew up in a place called Washington Crossing where George Washington and his troops crossed the Delaware River on that cold Christmas night in 1776. I had told him I worked my high school summers at the Washington Crossing State Park, New Jersey. Jack knew a little about Washington crossing the Delaware, but I was able to tell him the hardship Washington and his men went through crossing the Delaware River and winning the Battle of Trenton. I explained to him that I fished the river and swam in it since I was six years old.

I also told Jack how my twin and I would battle for the best Fourth of July poster and we would ride our decorated bikes in the kids bike parade when we were younger. When we were a little older, we were part of the Fourth of July Boat Show for a number of years. My twin and I and one of our friends dressed up in clown

96

outfits and rode on a six-foot round disk and our friend would climb up on our shoulders as we were pulled behind a boat.

After we learned how to ski better, we became a part of the Water Ski Show, that included both pyramids, and crisscrossing on slalom skis. This was all held in front of the Titusville Grammar School, where I attended school from kindergarten through sixth grade and where our Father took us for hitting practice, and where I took my three children to practice as well.

After the boat show there would be boat races, with an ending of a boat parade with all the local boats. When it got dark there were fireworks. Sometimes we would boat up to the Washington Crossing Bridge and watch the fireworks from the piers of the bridge. It meant a lot to me because I lived in the heart of how we became a free nation.

I also told Jack that every Christmas since 1953 reenactments were held where George Washington and his twenty-four hundred men, two hundred horses, and sixteen cannons crossed on that cold winter night on December 25th, 1776. At the time of the crossing there were two ferries that were big enough to carry both horse and carriage. It even carried the "Flying Machine" a coach that could travel in one day from New York City to Philadelphia, an amazing speed for its day. Ref. 22

Since I lived just up the street from the Crossing, I went to a number of the reenactments and on a couple of them I helped pull the boats to shore.

Jack told me how he, his friends Scott and Dennis, and sometimes a few other guys would fish and swim in the Boone River before a game. Often, he would canoe or raft down the river with a friend or two.

One of Jack's favorite fishing spots on Boone River.

Boone River Watershed is designated as a Protected Water Area and has a drainage area of approximately 908 miles. It is often utilized for recreation, such as canoeing, rafting, and fishing. The watershed has over 760 miles of streams that support a diversity of fish and wildlife species, including the federally endangered species Topeka Shiner. It was a great place to go on a hot day. Ref. 23

Jack asked if the letter from an ex-girlfriend was from the one that wanted me to desert and run to Canada to get married. I told him no; it was from a girl I dated for a while that was in the high school band with me and broke my heart when we broke up. She was my first love. Jack said he understood about a broken heart.

When in high school I was first trumpet in the school's marching band and orchestra. I worked my way to the number one chair because I practiced every day since seventh grade. I even played taps on Memorial Day, at some Veteran's funerals, and played the Star-Spangled Banner at some events. Jack was as impressed as I was about all the sports teams he played on while he was in high school.

Jack received a letter from a girl he dated since seventh grade named Pam Bert. He never talked much about her saying they ended up going to different colleges, Pam to Iowa State and Jack to Wartburg College, which were more than a hundred miles apart. He said, they just drifted apart. I could tell he was upset by what had happened, since he didn't talk much about her. It may have been why he understood about a broken heart.

He did tell me that in high school she was a football cheerleader, was the senior attendant with him for their homecoming, was part of the All-State Quartet Team with his friend Scott, and that she had a younger sister named Mary. I thought it better not to push it so I only let him bring her up when he felt like it and I did not talk about my broken heart. We may have had another thing in common.

We did talk a lot about the war and the many protests back at home. We were both against the war. Jack may not have been against it at first, but by this time he had seen that the war was wrong. We didn't like that we would go into an area, secure it for a while, then just give it back to the VC, and sometimes we ran low on supplies and water. We realized that the Vietnamese people were only fighting for their own land and country; something both Jack and I would have done if our country were invaded, plus the little kids were so darn cute. They reminded me of my younger sisters and brother, and reminded Jack of the neighborhood children that he included in his games, as well as his niece, Kim Arens.

We both thought we were defending America. I was always against the war but, felt I was doing my duty for my country. I used the sacrifices of those brave men that crossed that ice-coated river on a snowy cold Christmas night where I lived, for inspiration and to always do my very best.

During Advanced Infantry Training a spec-six who had already spent his year in Vietnam tried to force me from being against the war. He took me into his room in our barracks one night and made me do pushups and sit ups, trying to make me say I was for the war. I am not sure how many pushups and sit ups I ended up doing but I never agreed to be for the war. The next day he made me platoon sergeant of our training unit.

During Advanced Infantry Training, in the state of Washington, each morning while being trucked to our training for the day, I would look at Mount Rainier and think about, out over the mountain far off, is home. Many mornings the mountain would stand out in the eastern sky with incredible views. The mountain would reflect the morning sun, casting oranges and reds across the sky. I missed home, being on my own, knowing I would be heading to Vietnam. I thought the war was wrong but little was under my control.

One night Jack asked me why I did not play baseball in high school when my older brother played and got drafted by the Minnesota Twins. I told him my twin and I did play Little League, Babe Ruth, and junior high baseball but not high school. The rule was at the time that if you turned nineteen before the season you were too old to play on the high school team. Our birthday was February ninth so we turned nineteen before the baseball season of our senior year.

I did tell him that my older brother and I played on the same team in Little League. My older brother played shortstop and I played center field when I was eleven and he was twelve. We were undefeated that year and my next year. He led the league in homeruns his last year and I had the second most the following year. My twin Rich played shortstop for another Little League team.

Jack told me he played shortstop throughout his junior high and high school years, his friend Dennis Hoffman played third base, and Scott Case, another close friend, played center field and batted 3rd or 4th. Because he was fast, Jack was the leadoff hitter. He also told me Scott and Jack were so close they called each other's parents Mom and Dad. Dennis lived across the street from Jack.

To sleep at night, we had to crawl into a small metal half-moon-shaped bunker. It was tight, but provided some protection in case of incoming. One night, after being relieved from watch by Jack, I worked my way into it, and was ready to fall asleep when I felt something crawling on my chest. I quickly sat up, hitting my head. Suddenly, three sharp stings burned their way down my chest, almost paralyzing me, and I felt as if a 100-pound weight was pressing down on my chest. Finally, the pain let up. Somehow, a scorpion had found its way into the bunker. Lucky for me it was only a small one.

Every night, a little before dusk, we would arm the Claymore Mines by placing a small blasting cap into a small hole on the top. The blasting cap was attached to a wire that ran back to a hand clapper. By pressing a lever on the clapper, a small electric charge would be generated. The electric charge would travel along the wire, triggering the blasting cap, which in turn would set off the Claymore. Ref. 24

A Claymore has 700 metal balls in the killing zone.

We had gotten used to arming the Claymores. We always carried our own and would use them on night ambushes. So, we kind of took them for granted until an accident happened.

We had been on the mountain for about a week when there was a large explosion. We could hear someone screaming, but could not see from our position who it was or what had happened. We were not sure if it was incoming, or what, so we rushed to the bunker to be ready if we were being attacked.

A little later, we got a call on the radio that there was an accidental detonation of one of the Claymore Mines when it was being armed. Luckily, for the guy who was arming the Claymore, he was standing behind it. If he was standing in front, he would have been killed. Instead, his tour was over and he would have to live without a leg below his right knee and only part of his left foot. I guess it was a small price to pay for his life.

The arming of the Claymores became an adventure after that. You would stand alongside the Claymore so that if it misfired, you would only have your eardrums damaged instead of losing your legs or being killed.

Finally, the two weeks came to an end. As the Chinook helicopter landed to return us to the jungle below, I could not help but feel satisfied I had used up fourteen more days.

It was disappointing to leave the mountain. It was cool, somewhat secure, and you could see for miles. But we never got back to that mountain top, even though we were supposed to rotate up there every other month. Instead, we spent weeks on end hunting Charlie through the jungles, never knowing where the next mission was taking us, or when.

Robert M. Braun, Sr.

The Tunnels

It was March 11th and I was writing home about my last mission. My unit had just gotten off the mountain and had spent the last five days working on building hooches at FSB Kien.

It was good to get back out in the bush, it was a lot better than slaving under the hot sun to build hooches that may not be used much. We received orders that we were heading out for another five-day mission. I had to get ready so I couldn't finish the letter. On the fifth, my unit was flown out to set up night ambushes.

Hooch we helped build.

We had just gotten a new C O (Commanding Officer) and had been spending a lot more time out in the field; hunting through the endless jungle searching for Charlie. We were supposed to be resupplied on the third day out, but the new C O refused the resupply. By the end of the day, we had almost run out of water.

While the squad was stopped in a holding area, my buddy Jack and I gathered up the canteens and worked our way to a nearby stream to refill them. We were walking slowly down a well-used trail watching our every step. We then took a smaller trail that went right that led us to a small stream. We had our M-16s in the ready position on semi-automatic as we walked down the trail to the stream. We stopped a couple times to check the area and listen to the sounds of the jungle. It was hot and steamy, sweat poured off of Jack and me and the damn mosquitoes wouldn't leave us alone. Clouds of them flew around both of us.

When Jack and I reached the stream, I stood watch while Jack filled the canteens. We were lucky, we didn't see anything but both knew we could have run into VC at any time, since the area was being used by someone.

When we got back to the squad with the water, we made sure we put iodine tablets in the canteens. While we were in the holding area Lieutenant Sparks got a call on the radio that a VC base camp may be nearby and my squad was ordered to go try to find it.

Here we go again, heading off into the jungle now in search for a Viet Cong base camp. With Jack in the lead, with me close

102

behind, we traveled down a well-used trail, jungle on both sides. Added to the list of things to look for were red ant nests in the trees.

On a previous mission we ran into a nest of red ants and were sore for a few days from multiple ant bites, so we moved slowly down the trail looking for snipers, booby traps, snakes, and red ant nests. After walking down the trail for a while we ran into another trail that had fresh footprints. The trail ended splitting into two. Jack was told to check the right branch and I the left.

We returned to Lieutenant Sparks to report we didn't find anything. Lieutenant Sparks pointed to his right and if you looked really hard you could see a well camouflaged bunker. After finding the trail to the base camp, where we found a few booby traps, we reached the bunkers, found some tunnels, and reported we had found the VC base camp. As we crept down the trail to the bunkers, I yelled to Jack to stop. I saw a tripwire between Jack's feet that led to a grenade. Luckily for both of us, I saw the wire before the booby trap was set off; it may have killed both of us.

There were **eight most dangerous booby traps** used by the Viet Cong, they included: Punji Sticks, Grenade, Cartridge, Snake Pits, The Mace, Tiger, Pressure Release, and Bamboo Whip Traps. The one we mostly dealt with was the Grenade booby trap that were mostly found around tunnels, base camps, or near streams. Let me tell you a little about the booby traps soldiers serving in Vietnam may have had to encounter. Ref. 25

Grenade: A wire or string would be tied to the pin of the grenade and then tied to a tree or stick in the ground across the trail. When the wire or string was walked into, the wire or string pulled out the pin of the grenade and boom, the grenade goes off.

Grenades inside of cans: They were another way grenades were used as booby traps. The pins of the grenade would be pulled and then placed in cans with a wire connected fastened low to the ground or tree to the other side of a path. When the grenade is pulled from the can releasing the safety lever the grenade goes off.

Punji Sticks: The most infamous booby traps were the Punji Sticks. They were responsible for two percent of the wounds to American soldiers. Bamboo was mostly used in different lengths and widths, sharpened

103

at one end. The bamboo were sometimes smeared with urine, human waste, or plant poison and placed in areas that would be used by troops. The Punji Sticks in the pits were usually meant not to kill but to slow down a unit and were mostly in areas with tunnels or used in preparation for an ambush.

Cartridge: A small arms bullet was placed into a bamboo tube over a nail. When stepped upon, the bullet would be forced down on the nail igniting the primer and go off.

Snake Pits: Snake Pits were mostly found in tunnels. A snake was hidden inside a bamboo stick and would be released by a tripwire. Most often poisonous snakes were put in the bamboo sticks. The snakes were called "three step snakes" because the soldier bitten would only be able to take three steps due to the poisonous venom. The "Tunnel Rats" received special training to disarm these traps. Often snakes were placed in packs and sometimes tied to a branch by their tail at eye level.

The Mace: This was one of the worst booby traps. A wooden or metal ball with spikes would be tied to a tree and would be released by a tripwire to swing down from the tree striking the soldier.

Tiger: This trap was like the Mace Trap. But instead of a wooden or metal ball, a board would be connected to a tripwire, when tripped, would release the board or plank with metal spikes.

Pressure Release: The American soldier liked to capture NVA or Viet Cong flags. The Viet Cong knew this. So, they would not only booby trap important military items they would also use flags rigged with explosives. A secondary booby trap was usually set up so when an injured soldier was rushed to, a delayed charge would go off.

Bamboo Whip: A tripwire would be attached to a long bamboo pole with spikes all over it that would be pulled back into an arc. The bamboo pole whipped back impaling the soldier.

Back to the story.

Once we reached the bunkers, Jack and I were told to throw hand grenades into one of the bunkers. After the smoke cleared, I went down into the bunker with a platoon sergeant to check it out.

There were two tunnel entrances. He went down the tunnel entrance that went right and I went into the tunnel that went left.

After going down the tunnel maybe five meters I turned around because it got too dark to get some matches. We didn't bring flashlights, because we didn't expect to be going down into tunnels. The one good thing about the tunnel was, it was a cool relief from the hot sun. When I got back to the entrance the platoon sergeant was already back from his tunnel saying his tunnel came to an end.

After getting some matches we headed back down the tunnel that went left with me in the lead. The tunnel was small; we had to crawl on our hands and knees. After traveling down the tunnel maybe ten meters, I lit a match. The tunnel dropped down into another tunnel that went deeper.

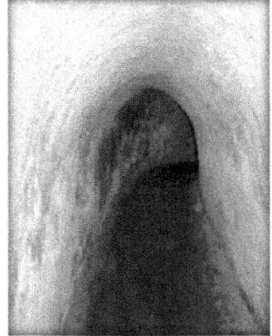

We squeezed down the tunnel about fifteen meters, I lit another match. In front of me, about a foot away, was a canteen. I used my bayonet to check for booby traps. After not finding any, I picked up the canteen and it was full. Whoever lost the canteen may not be far away. Not wanting to go any further without a flashlight and only a bayonet, I told the platoon sergeant we better go back. We were not trained to go into tunnels like the Tunnel Rats.

I had heard of the Tunnel Rats in tunnels training when I was in Cu Chi the second week in Vietnam. I was told that during the Vietnam war volunteers from the combat engineers and infantry men from the US and Australian Armies were used to clear and destroy enemy tunnel complexes. Their motto was *Non Gratus Anus Rodentum,* (Latin for not worth a rat's ass). Ref. 26

The Tunnel Rats standard issues were either a M1991 pistol or M1917 revolver, bayonet, flashlight, and explosives. The men who volunteered were usually small, five-foot five

Tunnel entrance after being blown up.

inches or smaller. I was six foot tall so the tunnel was pretty tight. Since the only thing I had was a bayonet, I thought it best to turn around and go back. After struggling to turn around we made it to the surface, dirty and happy to see the sunlight.

After spending another day stomping around the hot jungle, we were flown back to FSB Kien. To my surprise there was a package waiting for me. Wow, I couldn't have been happier. It was the first package I received since arriving in Vietnam. Of course, Jack, Lopez, and Brownie wanted to know what I got and were right next to me as I opened the package.

Inside of the package I found five pairs of socks, a couple of paperback books, two cans of peanuts, and a big bag of chocolate chip cookies with a note. The note had written on it telling me that my seven-year-old sister, Carrie, helped make the cookies. A picture of my twin and me was also in the package. The guys really got a kick out of the picture. They couldn't believe there were two of me.

There was also a note from my younger brother Carl. He was ten years old and a real good kid. My twin and I always included him and his friends in our basketball and baseball games. He told me in the letter how he stood up to a bully in his new class. The bully was supposed to meet him after school for a fight.

My brother wrote that he showed up, but the bully did not. He also wrote that the bully hadn't bullied him since. It was good knowing my little brother could take care of himself. How I missed my sisters, brothers, twin, and family.

I told Jack and the other guys about my younger brother standing up to the bully and that we used to include him, in our baseball and basketball games. Jack said he included a kid named Craig Bergstrom, his two brothers Steve and Bob, the sons of his football and baseball coach, and other younger kids in his neighborhood in his games also, just like my twin and me.

That night we feasted on chocolate chip cookies and washed them down with a couple of beers. We couldn't drink too many beers because we were heading out tomorrow for another five-day mission and had guard duty at night.

Guard duty was easy. You were on for one hour with another guy; on guard duty I usually was with Jack. You could listen to music on the radio as long as it was played quietly. At around 2100 hours there would be what is called, Mad Minute, where you could test your weapon to make sure it was firing straight. Sometimes we would load the M-16 magazine with tracers. The night would light up with tracers flying out into the night. One night someone hit one

of the fifty-gallon barrels of napalm, that burst into flames shooting high into the sky lighting up the night. Because it was so bright you could light up a cigarette and not have to worry about hiding it. The normal practice was no smoking at night because it gives the VC a target. The little red glow could be seen a long way in the dark.

I couldn't finish the letter I started the 11th to tell home about my last mission, because we got orders we would be moving out later that afternoon for another five-day mission. At 1400 hours we were picked up by three choppers.

Robert M. Braun, Sr.

Swimming in the Saigon River

It was March 21st, just back from a four-day mission. I was writing home about the best mission I have been on since arriving in Vietnam. I got to swim in the Saigon River. It was better than spending two weeks on top of Black Virgin Mountain or stomping through the jungle searching for our enemy. On a mission a little before this one, I accepted the responsibility of crawling into an NVA/VC tunnel system at one of their base camps.

This assignment started much like most of the others. My platoon was picked up early by three helicopters. Jack and I followed the radioman and Lieutenant Sparks into the first chopper. Jack and I always sat at the doorway, our feet hanging out, ready to be the first to hit the ground.

We flew over the Saigon River and the jungle for a little while then were dropped off in an open area. The squad moved into the jungle with Jack leading and me close behind. It was going to be another hot humid day much like the day before and the next. It was the dry season with day after day of heat.

After walking for a short time, we stopped in a holding area to wait until an hour before dark before moving to our ambush site. There wasn't much to do to pass the time. Most of the guys would take naps, write home, read old letters, or in Jack's and my case and a few other guys, we read paperback books. We carried them in our backpacks along with C-rations, water in two canteens, grenades, claymore mines, insect repellent, toilet paper on our helmets or in our shirt pocket, ammo magazines for our M-16s, and anything else we needed for days in the jungle.

In my package, that I received from home, my mother included two books that had just come out. One of the books was the "Godfather" and the other was entitled "Sounder". Jack and I, plus a few of the other guys exchanged books received from home or bought at the PX. We would read them while in the holding areas, waiting for night ambushes, or back at the firebase, to relax and get ready for night watch or the next mission.

I kept the "Godfather" to read and gave Jack "Sounder". I wanted to read the "Godfather" because it was about a crime family from New York City not too far from my home. Jack wanted "Sounder" because it was about an African-American sharecropping family. He was from a farming community and knew quite a few members of his high school's club, Future Farmers of America (FFA).

A few months ago, after just getting to Vietnam, I wrote my Father telling him I was reading a few different books. During most of my school years I didn't work very hard. My Father didn't push us. He was more involved with helping my brothers and me in sports. My Mother was too busy trying to deal with all the chores raising nine children. The only reason I did some work in high school to get good grades, at least good enough, was to continue playing basketball. I always got good marks in my music classes because I loved playing the trumpet. I was number one trumpet in marching band and orchestra. The marching band helped me master the moves of the military: left face, right face, about face, and march as a unit.

Once I got into the Army, I began to take my lessons seriously. During the tests in Basic Training, I really worked hard to do my best. It must have worked because I was the outstanding trainee of my basic training cycle at Fort Dix, New Jersey, by having the highest combined scores in academic and physical tests. Jack told me he got a perfect five hundred on the physical tests. I just missed five hundred by a few points.

Another thing Jack and I had in common was our belief in religion. Jack was a member of the Church of Christ and I was Catholic. On Ash Wednesday on the 11th of February, we were at FSB Kien and were able to receive ashes. We knew Easter was approaching, a little more than a week away, and were hoping to be able to go to Easter Mass on the 29th of March. How I missed going to Easter Mass with my whole family, all dressed in our best. Easter would be another holiday we all would be away from our families.

I can still remember when my two brothers and I had our pictures taken before heading to Mass with our grandparents, and the one of my two brothers and three sisters and me. My Mother would always have our Sunday best ready to wear and we would have to take them off, and hang them up as soon as we got home.

We were a close family growing up in a safe environment and were free to wander and play in our neighborhood: where we played sandlot baseball in a friend's field, basketball on our dirt court in our backyard, and explored the woods near our home. We didn't have a lot of money but always had food on the table thanks mostly to our Grandfather, who was a barber and owned his own barbershop.

I remember going to our grandparent's home almost every Saturday morning to go into their basement to retrieve canned goods, cereals, soups, and other dry goods. Also, every Wednesday and Saturday evening my Grandmother and Grandfather would visit. They would bring popsicles for us and the other kids in the neighborhood, and on Saturday they brought some type of meat for Sunday dinner. Boy, did I miss my family, and found myself daydreaming about home, often.

Ok, back to our mission. At around 1900 hours we headed out to set up our ambush. It turned out to be a carbon copy of most of our ambushes. Two guys would be on an hour watch while the rest of the squad slept. Most of the time I had watch with Jack because we would be next to each other during the ambushes; like the many we had been on; we did not see anything.

This is not my unit but one like it.

The next morning around 0700 hours a chopper flew in breakfast and resupplied us with C-rations, ammo, and water, if we needed any. The breakfasts weren't too bad with scrambled eggs, bacon and sausage, pancakes, and hot coffee. We all knew that this may be our last warm breakfast in a while because our new commanding officer didn't always want to be resupplied so, we all ate our fill.

After breakfast and cleaning the area we headed down a trail that eventually led to the Saigon River. There waiting for us were three Patrol Boats.

The Patrol Boats were used to search and stop traffic in the areas of the Mekong Delta, Saigon River, and the Rung Sat Special Zone. They were assigned to the Task Force Clearwater, were used to try to stop shipments of weapons to our enemy, and were often in firefights with VC and NVA on shore and on boats.

Picture, I took when moving out on the river.

The Patrol Boats were manned by a four-man crew, a 1st Class Petty Officer that was the captain, a gunner, an engine man, and a seaman. Each man was cross-trained in each other's job.

A pair of them usually operated, and patrolled the waterways together, both in the command of the patrol officer. In our case there were three boats.

The Patrol Boats were fast and highly moveable, and could reach a speed of 28.5 knots or 32 mph and go in shallow water as little as two feet deep. Each boat was heavily armed with twin M2HB, two 50-caliber machine-guns, a single rear M2HB, one or two M60mm light machine-guns, one on the port and starboard side, and a MK19 grenade launcher. Ref. 27

Enemy bunkers were on shore and that was our assignment while on the boats to destroy as many bunkers as we could. It was why we brought along a few M72 LAW, a light anti-tank weapon. They were dropped off to my unit with the hot breakfast.

The M72 LAW was a portable one shot 66mm unguided solid rocket propulsion anti-tank weapon developed in 1959. I carried one, Jack got another, and Lieutenant Sparks had the third. Once we all were on the Patrol Boats we idled out to the middle, and then took off. We all had to hold onto the boats; they took off so fast. Being on the boats and on the river reminded me of being on the

Delaware River back home. I just wished there were skis so I could water ski behind the boats. Ref. 28

We were told that it would take about an hour before we got to the first VC/NVA base camp that needed to be destroyed. We flew up the river passing Vietnamese in sampans and other boats heading up and down the river. The Patrol Boats did slow some when going by them and we even got waves from some of the people in the boats.

After going by a few villages along the Saigon we entered the portion of the river that ran through the jungle and where we would be stopping to destroy a base camp. There was jungle on both sides and we slowed down to make less noise. We slowed to a stop and to our right we could see bunkers used by our enemy.

You could tell that the VC base camp had been bombed before, but still needed some more work to destroy some of the bunkers. The boats idled to keep from being pulled down the river by the current so we could use the weapons on the boat and the M72 LAWs we carried onboard.

Lieutenant Sparks was the first to fire the M72 LAW. He got down on his knees, ready to fire. He looked through the scope, his right hand on the firing mechanism and fired the M72.

A rocket shot out almost in slow motion. You could watch the rocket head to the nearest bunker and explode with a large bang and a fireball. We all

Picture, I took of Lieutenant Sparks firing the M72.

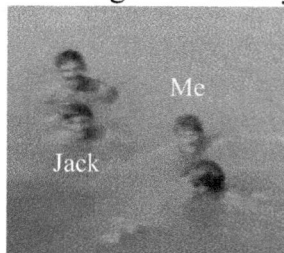

cheered and congratulated Lieutenant Sparks for a great shot. Jack fired his M72 next, at another bunker, and I followed after Jack to fire my M72. Then we moved to the M50 machine-gun to destroy the bunker some more. It was a lot more fun firing the M50 machine-gun on the boat than when on top of Black Virgin Mountain, when we thought we were under an attack.

After spending some time destroying the base camp we headed upriver for a while, and because we were way ahead of schedule, the boats ended

112

up pulling along the bank. It was another hot day so we went swimming. None of us had bathing suits so, we went naked.

It was about fifteen feet from the top of the cabin on the deck, to the river, so we were able to dive. Jack, a couple other guys, and myself did flips off the roof of the cabin. It was fun and we were

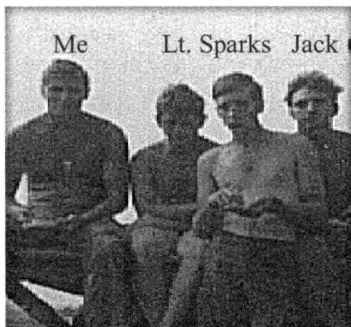

Me   Lt. Sparks   Jack

able to beat the heat for a while. It was the best time while serving in Vietnam and that is what I wrote home to tell my family. What a great day we had! When we were finished swimming, we sat on the roof of the cabin. I had brought one of the cans of peanuts, from the package I received from home with me, and we all had a few. It was a great day! We were able to swim a little, cool off, and almost forget we were in a war zone.

The good time had to come to an end so a short time later, we headed back up the river and were dropped off near the Michelin Rubber Plantation, back in the war and back to hunting Charlie.

The Michelin Rubber Plantation was located almost half way between the Cambodian border and about 72 km northwest of Saigon. Because of its' location it was an important staging area for the Viet Cong.

The Michelin Rubber Plantation.

The rubber plantation was established in 1925, the largest rubber plantation in Vietnam, and one of the major sources of revenue for the South Vietnam Government. Ref. 29

There were a number of operations against the PAVN (The People's Army of Vietnam) and the VC in and around the rubber plantation. In 1965 the ARVN (The Army of the Republic of Vietnam) 7th Regiment and the U.S. 5th Division were overrun by the VC, killing most of the ARVN Regiment, and 5 U.S. advisers. In February 1966 Operation Mastiff conducted a search and destroy mission, in the Dau Tieng District of Vietnam.

In February 1967 another operation, called Junction City was carried out. It was an eighty-two-day military operation conducted by the United States and the Republic of Vietnam. It was the first

U.S. combat airborne operation since the Korean War and one of the largest Airmobile Operations of the war. The 3rd Brigade, 25th Infantry conducted Operation Diamond Head in December 1967. In August and September of 1968 Operation Phase III Offensive was held, and the plantation was the scene of heavy fighting during and after the 1968 Tet Offensive. The last operation in the rubber plantation was called Operation Atlas Wedge that occurred in March 1969, (Binh Duong Province), about a year before my unit entered the Michelin Rubber Plantation.

After we got off the boats, we were all in good moods, and started into the rubber plantation making way too much noise, because a short way down a trail, we heard a voice telling us to halt. Another unit was in a holding area, had heard us, and were not sure who was making all the noise. Lucky for us they heard us speaking English.

After talking to the other unit, we headed to a holding area a few miles away from the river. The next few nights we set up night ambushes in the rubber plantation and like so many other nights, we didn't see anything.

One day, while in the rubber plantation, we didn't have to battle the VC, but snakes. We were in a holding area and wanted to get out of the sun so, Jack and I crawled under some bushes. When we got under the bushes, we saw a couple of long green snakes at the top. Not knowing if they were poisonous or not, Jack and I took our M-16s and shot them. It seemed like there was always something we had to look out for and battle.

Once back in FSB Kien we were informed that our unit would be guarding the road to FSB Kien and its' water supply for the next week or so. Easter was only a little over a week away and our unit had been out for almost ten straight days. It was great news to all of us, and sounded a lot easier than walking through the hot, insect, and snake infested jungle.

Robert M. Braun, Sr.

Guarding the Waterhole and Road

It was March 26th, 1970. For the last few days, my squad had been patrolling the road to FSB Kien, for the purpose of making a safe route for the daily resupply caravan, and guarding the waterhole that was used to help supply FSB Kien with water. We had been spending a lot of time in the field and finally were given some "out of the jungle" assignments.

It was almost three and a half months since arriving in Vietnam, only a little over eight and a half months to go. The responsibility of road guard duty was a lot better assignment and a break from stomping around in the jungle.

Each morning, we would meet the minesweepers at 0600 hours at the main gate. They had been trained how to use the PRS-7 Portable Mine Detecting Set.

"The PRS-7 detector is used to detect both metallic and non-metallic mines. The head contains a fixed frequency oscillator which drives a pair of transmit antennas 180 degrees out of phase by means of a BALUN transformer. The receiving antenna is located at the null between the two transmit antennas and normally has a small output. But when there is distortion of the transmit balance, like by the presence of a mine the output increases. All the op amps are 709 powered by +15 and -15 Volts. All the signal processing is analog." Ref. 30

My unit's responsibility was to protect the minesweepers and so far we had not guarded the waterhole after walking guard. While some of the unit was guarding the minesweepers and the road, others would guard the waterhole. When on road duty we would sometimes hang out in one of the villages along the road.

On the second day of duty one of the minesweepers detected something in the road. Jack and I would be following a short distance behind, along with a few other members of our unit, with our M-16s in the ready position. We didn't have to carry our normal amount of equipment, just canteens for water, some C-rations, a bayonet, a few hand grenades on our ammo belt, and magazines for our M-16s.

Robert M. Braun, Sr.

The M67 grenade weighs 14 oz. (400 grams) in total and has a safety clip to prevent the spoon on the grenade from being triggered in the event the safety pin is accidentally pulled. The safety pin prevents the safety lever, or "spoon" on the grenade from moving and releasing the spring-loaded striker which initiates the grenade's fuze assembly. It contains 6.5 oz. of composition B explosives, and a M213 delay fuze. Ref. 31

The grenade M67 was shaped like a baseball so it was called the Baseball Grenade. It could be thrown by an average male soldier ninety-eight to one hundred fifteen feet; with a delay of between four to five seconds after the release of the spoon. The steel fragments had an injury radius of about ninety-eight feet and a kill radius of around sixteen feet. Because both Jack and I had pretty good arms we always carried at least a few.

After we were told about something suspicious being found in the road, either Jack or I would check it out. I volunteered. Everyone moved back while I knelt down near the area that set off the PRS-7 detector, and used my bayonet to probe around the area. Sure enough, I hit something solid, gently moved the dirt from the area, and found a landmine. It was removed and taken to an out of the way place and blown up.

There were a number of different mines the VC would use. One the Vietnamese used was like the American's M14 mine called the MD-82. The only difference between the two was that the MD-82 used a fuzing system. If stepped upon, it was a type of pressure device that would explode. Ref. 32

A fuze device was what detonates the explosive material under certain conditions and they normally would have a safety, and arming mechanisms that were used to protect the user.

The smaller mines were called *dap loi* step-mine, and the *min muoi* or mosquito mine, were used by the North Vietnamese. 65-70% of American deaths were caused by mines and booby traps in 1965 alone. The Vietnamese civilian population were often casualties and amputees, caused from American landmines and VC or NVC landmines and/or booby traps. Ref. 33

116

Robert M. Braun, Sr.

I can still remember seeing a young child struggling to return home with the lower part of their right leg missing, from some kind of landmine or booby trap, that tore off the child's lower leg. My heart still bleeds from the memory.

Picture, I took of squad sergeant who went into the tunnels with me.

Picture, I took of some of my unit with the kids.

One day while in a village Jack, me, and some of the guys in my unit got to hang around with some of the Vietnamese children. We were friendly with them and gave them candy to show our friendship. They reminded me of my younger brother and sisters and, reminded Jack of the kids in his neighborhood, along with his little niece Kim Arens. They were so cute. Jack had told me earlier that he told his niece, before he was shipped out, that he would return from Vietnam with both legs or not at all.

I thought it was a strange thing to say, so I asked Jack why he said it, and asked if he had a dream, like I did after a high school basketball game, that I was in a firefight in Vietnam. He said he did not have a dream; it was just something he said. Because I had his back, and he had mine, I tried to do everything I could to make sure Jack and I both returned home with two legs. It was one of the many reasons I volunteered to walk point with him, and to check out the landmine. I would have done the same things for my twin and my friends. Jack would have done the same things for his friends.

The next few days flew by. Finally on the twenty-ninth, Easter, Jack, me, and a few other guys were assigned to guard the waterhole. We could go to an early Easter Mass and have some of Jack's Easter candy, which he received in a package when we got back from road duty on the twenty-eighth. Like we did whenever one of us got a package, we shared.

After an early Easter Mass and breakfast, we headed down to the waterhole with jelly beans in our pockets. We headed out the main gate and walked down the road to the pond following the

117

---

minesweepers. The pond was just off the road near a bridge that went over a small stream. At the far end of the pond, were woods where the stream disappeared into the overgrowth. The pond was about a half-acre in size, and at one end, may have been ten feet deep; with long weeds growing around part of it with some trees along the banks hanging over the waterhole. It reminded me of a few of the ponds I fished at home.

I thought back about the time when my three brothers and I were fishing a small pond not too far from home in the Washington Crossing State Park, New Jersey. My twin and my older brother were fishing at one end, and I was with our eight-year-old brother, Carl.

We got to an area where I had caught some nice Large Mouth Bass in the past. I let Carl use my fishing pole to fish the area and told him to retrieve the plastic worm really slowly, as if he had a bass looking at the worm. He did as he was told and sure enough he caught a nice Large Mouth Bass. My twin and older brother kept shouting snag because Carl's pole was bending so much. They couldn't believe our little brother caught the fish of the day.

I was right there to help; not sure I had ever seen him so happy; he was smiling ear to ear. Maybe this was the first time he competed with his older brothers, and won! How I missed my family.

After the road was checked, Jack, Lopez, me, and a few of the newer guys moved back to the waterhole to spend the day. It was going to be another hot day and the water looked really inviting. We found a good place to stay out of the sun and somewhat concealed but, could still keep an eye on the waterhole and road.

Some new recruits had just become members of our unit. They were inexperienced, and not from the country, but from cities like New York, Chicago, Miami, and didn't know the woods like Jack and me. Some spoke Spanish; we were learning a little of it from them, and we tried to help them learn to survive in this harsh country, that harbored dangers at every turn.

It was 0730 hours when we got back to the waterhole. It was warm and we knew it would be getting warmer, and the warmer it got the more inviting the pond looked.

We carried our normal array of equipment for guarding the road and waterhole: the M-16, ammo for it, hand grenades, canteens for water, a bayonet, some C- Rations, and the jelly beans.

There were twelve different types of C-Rations or Combat Rations that came in a rectangular box that included one large and two small cans. A brown foil accessory pack and white plastic spoon were in clear plastic. The meals contained about twelve hundred calories and weighed around two and a half pounds.

Each box was labeled with the type of meal. Some of the twelve meals included; chicken or turkey loaf, beefsteak, beans with frankfurter chunks, and spaghetti with meatballs in tomato sauce. My favorite was the spaghetti and meatballs and Jack's was the beans with frankfurters.

Each package came with a bread unit that came in three different varieties; crackers with two chocolate discs, either crème or coconut, four hardtack biscuits, cookie sandwich or fudge disc.

The last food in C-Rations was dessert: either canned fruit, pound cake, fruitcake, or cinnamon nut roll; along with the accessory pack which contained pepper, salt, sugar, instant coffee, non-dairy creamer, two pieces of chewing gum, toilet paper, a pack of four cigarettes, and a book of 20 moisture-proof matches.

The most important thing in the package were four P-38 can openers. They were small and easily lost. Without one, it was difficult to open the cans. Ref. 34

As we sat around, we talked about home like we always did. Jack told me more about the time he went to a sports camp known as the Fellowship of Christian Athletes, at Estes Park, Colorado and climbed a mountain called "Teddy's Teeth". He said he was with his friend Scott Case, Coach Wayne Bergstrom, and professional football players: Fran Tarkenton, Bobby Timberlake, Ken Hatfield, and other athletes. They all held hands and sang *"How Great thou Art"*. Jack tried to sing it but, he had a really bad voice.

Jack told me that he had Coach Bergstrom as a teacher in Middle School for Math and Social Studies. He said he would often see him at Little League fields or football games with his three sons.

Sometimes he would talk to Jack and tell him he saw him play and was impressed with some of his plays at shortstop. He also told him to practice bunting because he was fast. Other times he told him he made a nice run or pass in a football game. Jack said he knew all three sons because he, Dennis and Scott used to include them in neighborhood baseball or football games. Most likely, Coach Bergstrom was scouting for what was coming up from the youth programs to his high school football and baseball teams, since he was the coach for both. Jack ended up playing varsity football and baseball for Coach Bergstrom, basketball, all four years he was in high school, and was also on the track and golf teams. He lettered in all five sports.

Jack told me Coach Bergstrom was one of the biggest positive influences in his life. I thought I would take this time to give you some more information about Coach Bergstrom since, he helped Jack, to become the man Jack became, a Leader.

Coach Bergstrom obituary:

Wayne Bergstrom, 81, of Montgomery, Texas, formerly of Clarion and Des Moines, Iowa, passed away Saturday, October 26, 2013 after a valiant battle against cancer. Wayne was born on August 1, 1932 in Des Moines, Iowa. He grew up on the East Side and was always proud that he was an East Sider and was often heard saying, "Lee Township against the World". He graduated in 1950 from East High School, and attended Iowa State Teachers College for one year before transferring to Drake University where he starred in baseball, playing second base. During his junior year he was named the most valuable player of his Bulldog team. Wayne was the first member of his family to attend college. After graduating from Drake, he married the love of his life, Jean Molsberry on June 18, 1954. Wayne served in the Army from 1955-56 and then followed his dream of becoming a teacher and a coach with his first position at Bridgewater-Fontanelle High School. Then he took a position as head football coach at Clarion High School where he would successfully coach until 1971 when he became athletic director until assuming that same position at Ballard High School in 1981. He and Jean then moved to Montgomery, Texas in 1996 following his retirement. Wayne had many passions in life but his number one was family. He and Jean raised three boys in Iowa and their life revolved around them from family vacations to kids sports, golfing, and his beloved Iowa State Cyclones. Wayne touched thousands of lives in ways only they may know through teaching, coaching, and serving his communities. He received the Distinguished Service Award in 1963 from the Clarion Community and also started the Fellowship of Christian Athletes in Clarion in the early 1960's. Following his retirement, he spent a great deal of his time supporting his Montgomery County Salvation Army. He was also an active member of the First United Methodist Church of Conroe, Texas. Wayne will be remembered for his gentle soul, fierce spirit, quick wit, and infectious laugh. All who were fortunate enough to share his path along the way will truly miss him. He is survived by his loving and devoted wife of 59 years, Jean, three sons, Steve (Debbie), of Woodlands, Texas, Craig (Rhonda), of Johnston, Iowa, and Bob (Kathy), of Littleton, Colorado; 8 grandchildren, and 4 great-grandchildren. Wayne was preceded in death by his loving mother, Lillie in 1979. A Celebration of Life Service will be held on Thursday, October 31 at 2:00 pm at the First United Methodist Church in Conroe, Texas. In lieu of flowers, memorials may be made to the Montgomery County Salvation Army, PO Box 897, Conroe, Texas 77305 marked: In memory of Wayne Bergstrom. (The aforementioned obituary was written by Wayne's son Craig in honor of his Father.)

Eulogy for Wayne Bergstrom
by Craig Bergstrom

For those of you who do not know me, I am the proud middle son of Wayne and Jean Bergstrom. This is my first attempt at a eulogy so I apologize if I stumble along the way. I also want to tell you that I represent my two brothers, Steve and Bob who would love to tell you what Dad meant to them, but did not feel they could get through it. Not sure I can either but here goes.

To some he was Mr. Bergstrom, to others he was Wayne. To many he was Coach. To those friends closest to him, he was Bergie. To me he was Dad, and I could not have been more honored to call him that.

He was a simple man. He grew up on the East side of Des Moines which was not the best side of town. He was born in a Salvation Army hospital to a 20-year-old single mother in 1932.

He lived with his Swedish immigrant grandparents and his mother and he was always proud of his roots as an East Sider. You see, my dad never forgot where he came from. A passion for sports is what drove him and he played them morning, noon, and night. I'm not sure when during his life, he decided to be a coach but we are all fortunate that he made that choice.

If I was to describe my dad, I think it can be summed up in three letters: FFF. Family, Faith, and Football. Nothing mattered more to him than family. He met and married my mom in 1954 and for 59 years they had a partnership that most couples dream of. They were inseparable.

It was always Bergie and Jean. They were a perfect match. Dad was a glass half full kind of guy; Mom always thought the glass was half empty. Dad was a procrastinator, Mom wanted things done yesterday. But they shared common values, and beliefs in what is important in life and I admire my mom so much for the love and devotion she gave Dad for 59 years and especially through all the battles with his health over the past 10 years.

My dad loved a good laugh; afternoon naps; pasta for dinner; ice cream (which by the way was his last meal); golf (especially with his 3 boys); Cyclone victories; reading the sports page on the toilet; a cold beer, making Grandpa cards; watching his grandchildren in anything; the Big 12 tournament; traveling around the world; and Mom of course. He took us on family vacations all over the country when they had no money.

I have such great memories of the green cooler, packing the car top carrier, Coleman stove, eating cereal with milk right out of the boxes, Holiday Inns, swimming in the motel swimming pools, and baseball games....what a blast that was. Those trips sparked my love of history and brought us closer as a family.

Later in life we would go on golf trips together in places like Pebble Beach, Whistling Straights, the Old Course in St. Andrews, and Ireland. We loved every second of it especially at #3 at Whistling Straights in 2007 when Dad got his hole in one....at 75 years old.

Sports have always been at the core of our family, first playing them and then watching them...any of them. I loved being the son of the football coach. Dick Basham, Denny Bowman, Jerry Boyington, Jack Smith...those were my heroes when I was growing up in Clarion, Iowa.

Was my dad successful? If it is measured by wins or financial net worth, no. But real success is not measured by how much money you have or how many games you won, but by the impact you make on others' lives during your lifetime. Mac Willemssen from the class of 1965 said, "Coach was the true embodiment of what a high school coach should be. He cared about his players, set a good example, and was fun to be around. Bergie made us feel we were playing for a higher purpose when we played varsity football. He instilled the right values in us as young men."

He went on to share one of the special things that Coach Bergie did was start the local chapter of Fellowship of Christian Athletes and taking some of his players to FCA camps in places like Ashland, Oregon and Estes Park, Colorado. You see my dad always felt the job of a football coach was more than just teaching blocking and tackling.

It is easy to see after reviewing these, that Jack had many of Coach Bergstrom's characteristics like; gentle soul, fierce spirit, quick wit, a great laugh, and he is missed by many.

Back to the story.

Around 0830 hours Jack and I spotted two young boys walking on the road coming from a nearby village. They were carrying fishing poles made from long bamboo with a short line and hook. As soon as we saw them our eyes lit up. We both fished when back at home; Jack in the Boone River and me, in the Delaware River.

Jack had told me that Scott Case, Dennis Hoffman, he, and a few other guys, sometimes fished and swam in the Boone River on days of games during the Summer. He also told me he fished with his friends at local ponds, and I told him I did the same.

The Boone River is one hundred and eleven miles long, drains into the watershed that eventually feeds into the Mississippi River, and is a tributary of the Des Moines River. A stretch Jack liked the most cuts through a wooded valley that is good for canoeing and fishing. The types of fish included Small Mouth Bass, Channel Catfish, Walleye, Northern Pike, and Flathead Catfish. Ref. 23

We watched the two kids fish for a while and saw they were only catching small fish. Neither Jack nor I knew what kind they were. Jack opened one of his C-Rations and took out a few of the frankfurter chunks. We walked down to where the kids were fishing to see if we could bribe them to let us use one of the poles. It took most of our jelly beans to get a pole. Jack took one of the chunks of frankfurter and put it on the hook and said come on, and we walked to the deeper end.

It didn't take long before Jack had a fish interested in the frankfurter. Suddenly, Jack pulled back on the pole; he had a big one. The kids ran over, were clapping their hands, saying something in Vietnamese. Sure enough, Jack pulled out a big fish about a foot and a half long.

We didn't know what kind it was, but it had a large mouth with a lot of teeth, and had a long dorsal fin on the top of its back. We ended up catching a few more before running out of frankfurters. The kids loved the fish and took them home. Later, we found out that the fish were Snakeheads and were a favorite of the Vietnamese people.

This is not Jack, but just like how he dove into the pond.

After the kids left, it was getting really warm and the pond looked like a good place to cool off. So, we went to the pond. I was standing on the side and Jack dove straight in. I was glad I didn't go right in, like Jack, because he came out with a bunch of leeches on him. We used insect repellent to get the leeches off. We all had a good laugh.

After we got all the leeches off, we went back to our holding area to get something to drink and eat our lunch of C-Rations. I didn't drink much and Jack asked why I never drank much water.

I told him, when growing up, my home often ran out of water in the summer. We had our own well that supplied us with water but it was not deep enough and ran dry almost every year.

My father, brothers, and I had to go to the Washington Crossing State Park, New Jersey, each morning with a bunch of gallon glass water bottles to get water for the day. My mother used the water for cooking and we all used the water for bathing and flushing the toilet with the bath water. All of us kids used the same water for bathing. So, I learned early to use less water after hearing my father tell all of us many, many times, not to waste water.

We finally got our well dug deeper from the money my parents received from the law suit filed against the school where Rich almost had his left hand cut off. We found out that the school had dumped broken bottles behind the bleachers. With a deeper well we didn't have to lug the water bottles anymore and had plenty of water to make my mother's life easier. Jack was impressed and could see why I shared so much and was a good teammate.

The day dragged by. Throughout the day we watched the people from the nearby villages travel up and down the road; many walking or riding bikes, on oxen carts, and a few in three-wheel cars, along with military vehicles.

Around 1800 hours we were back at FSB Kien. We unloaded our gear and headed to the mess hall for dinner. When it got a little darker, we headed to the bunkers for our one-hour night watch.

While we were resting before night watch, Lieutenant Sparks received orders that the next day, March 30th, we would have the day off to rest and get ready for a sweep and destroy mission on the thirty-first.

Robert M. Braun, Sr.

This is my third and final story about Vietnam that was published in a national magazine in the late 1990s.

With Me Still

The date was March 31st, 1970. I had been in Vietnam for almost four months, stationed with the 2nd battalion, 12th Infantry, 25th Infantry Division and stationed at FSB Kien. It was early morning, and my platoon was on the chopper pad, waiting to be flown out to the jungle for a sweep-and-destroy mission.

Leaving FSB Kien

My platoon was the last of the company to be picked up for this mission. The other two platoons had been flown out earlier to set up. We were the pushers. Ideally, we were to push the Viet Cong into the other two platoons. The Viet Cong were supposed to hear us, run away, and then be ambushed by our main force as they disappeared into the jungle.

Standing on the chopper pad that morning, all of us were in good moods. It was payday and it was supposed to be an easy mission. We had just gotten back from a week in the bush and then guarding the road and waterhole for FSB Kien, and would have some money and time to relax after completing this assignment.

I stood on the LZ and talked to the squad's radioman, Lieutenant Sparks, and Jack, with whom I had developed a close friendship. We volunteered to share the point position for the first squad and had walked it for almost two months. We worked together like a well-oiled machine and quickly became the best in our company.

Brownie and Jack
I took the picture.

He would look for booby traps while I searched the trees for snipers and also checked for booby traps, two working as one. We were all dressed in jungle fatigues, fully armed with hand grenades and ammo. A number of us had M-16 rifles. Two men carried M-60 machine guns, one for each squad, with Brownie in mine, and a few others were armed with

127

M-79 grenade launchers. We did not pack our normal load of food and water, since we all were expected to be back later that day.

As we stood there, our radioman cautioned Jack and me to be careful. He told us that he had received reports that the enemy had been spotted in the area we were being flown into. But Jack and I still did not expect to see the Viet Cong.

We heard helicopters in the distance. Soon four choppers appeared. They quickly descended, banked right, and landed on the LZ. Dust flew as Lieutenant Sparks and the radioman climbed into one side of the first chopper. Jack and I followed. As usual, we sat in the doorway, our feet hanging out the door, ready to be the first ones out. Everyone was quiet as the chopper lifted off the LZ and headed into the jungle. We made a hard left-hand turn and I held on tightly, remembering the time Jack had grabbed onto me as I was sliding out of the chopper.

As I sat looking down at the treetops, thoughts of my family began to run through my mind. My family was large, nine children: five girls and four boys. I was the third, born nine months and one day after the oldest boy and ten minutes after my identical twin brother. This was my first time away from home, my family, my twin. I spent the hours and days in Nam trying to picture what they were doing back in the States. The hardest thing was being away from my twin. It was like a part of me was missing.

As I look back, I see that my friend, Jack, had taken my twin brother's place in my life. He was a lot like my twin: tough, determined, hardworking, unafraid to stand up for what he believed, and most important of all, compassionate. Jack and I developed a friendship and closeness that I will cherish for the rest of my life.

It took about ten minutes for us to be flown to our drop-off point. As the choppers began to move closer to the treetops, Jack and I began to scan the area for any signs of the Viet Cong. On a previous mission, smoke was spotted coming from a hedgerow. The squad had dropped in on Viet Cong preparing their breakfast. One, who did not disappear fast enough, never ate that breakfast, or any other.

As the choppers flew low, skimming the treetops, they made a lot of noise to signal the Viet Cong that we were there. We were soon dropped off, and split into two squads, with Jack and me leading the first.

As we prepared to move out, the radioman again cautioned us to be careful. Jack and I were confident, but concerned, and told the radioman not to worry.

In the past, almost every time we moved into a suspected Viet Cong stronghold, the enemy had gone. They would slip into the jungle or disappear through their complex tunnel systems. Our most successful method of destroying our enemy was night ambush, where we sat at night and waited for them to walk into our trap.

But, as of late, there had been an increase in enemy activity in the territory we now patrolled. About two weeks before, one of our helicopters was shot down, seriously injuring one of the crew. Also, a camp on top of Black Virgin Mountain that my platoon had just spent two weeks on, had been shelled with 45 mortar rounds.

The new region was thick jungle and bush. We had just taken over the area from the Big Red One and spent a lot more time out in the boonies on patrol. Luck had been on our side; our squad had not seen any action. But we all knew that it was just a matter of time before our luck changed.

We started cautiously down a well-used trail, thick jungle on both sides. Jack led, with me close behind. I scanned the tree line for snipers and other signs of Charlie. We proceeded very slowly, all senses on red alert, expecting to be confronted at any moment, but hoping that the enemy would flee as was usual. After walking for a little while, we came to a point where the trail branched off to form a Y. The area was scary. The air smelled of Charlie.

Just before the squad reached the Y, Jack and I moved back to the lieutenant and asked him which trail to go down. Lieutenant Sparks told Jack to check out the trail that branched left, while I was to check the right branch.

I started off, my senses ringing like a five-alarm fire. I thought about what my father had told me just before I left for Nam: he did not want a hero; he wanted his son back. I checked for signs of recent activity. My past experiences in the woods and fields around my home as a kid had taught me how to tell if footprints were fresh.

Moving down this trail, I saw many footprints that looked very fresh. I thought, *shoot to kill*! Then I came to a small opening in the jungle. That's when I spotted a sandal. It was the type used by the Viet Cong. I knew how important the homemade footwear was, whoever had been wearing it might still be around. I looked around the opening for other signs of the Viet Cong and then quickly returned to the squad with the sandal to report my findings.

Jack and Lieutenant Sparks agreed with me: the right branch of the Y should get a second look. We cautiously returned. Sweat poured off of me. The sun was now high in the cloudless sky. It was hot and steamy, and tension high. Our earlier confidence had turned into shaky hope that we would survive.

Jack and I crept down the right branch toward the opening. Charlie had been there or might still be there. The air smelled of fish and smoke, a sure sign the area was being used by the enemy. We were a short distance ahead of the rest of the squad, our M-16s on semi-automatic, and in the ready position. We inched forward, warily. We saw no signs of Charlie except fresh footprints.

Suddenly, about one third of the way into the opening, Jack and I heard a strange noise; a crack, that sounded like a round being chambered or a bullet flying overhead. We hit the ground at the same time and fired our M-16s toward the front left side of the opening. The VC had not run this time; they were there, waiting. We'd almost led our squad into a Viet Cong ambush.

There was no cover, nothing to hide behind. We were sitting ducks. Bullets hit all around us, shooting up puffs of dust as they hit the ground. I was on the ground, beside Jack, on his right side, and shot into the jungle hoping I was firing at the unseen enemy. The rest of the squad was behind Jack and me, also firing into the jungle and trying to move up to help us.

Jack rolled over on his left side, a hand grenade in his right hand. He looked at me and smiled, the one he always flashed when things got tough. As he attempted to throw the grenade, I felt a sharp burning sensation in my right bicep, and looked down to see a small hole in the sleeve on my jungle fatigues. I watched the color of my fatigues quickly change from green to red, and called for the medic.

At about the same time, Lieutenant Sparks shouted, Grenade! I instantly dove to my right, not really knowing the location of the grenade. I never felt myself land. Instead, I was floating in darkness with a bright light in the distance. Everything was peaceful as I moved closer to the light, drifting, drifting. I began to think about my family, my twin, and how much I would miss them. Fighting hard, I regained consciousness, and had no idea how long I had been unconscious.

My medic was working on me trying to stop the bleeding. I had shrapnel wounds in my right leg, back, groin, head, and a bullet wound in my right arm. My head injury caused me to drift in and out of consciousness as I fought the hardest fight of all… for my life!

Jack wasn't so lucky. That smile he gave me was the last time I ever saw my friend Jack, alive. Our friendship over the four months we were together, in extremely hard and dangerous times, where we had to live life in its most primitive state, has left an impression on me that drives me. Many, many times I have asked why I was given the gift of life and not Jack.

Once back in the states, I was able to obtain Jack's home address in   Iowa, and I wrote to his parents. I received a couple letters from Jack's father, Mr. Donald R. Smith. He told me how hard Jack's mother, family, and friends had taken the loss of Jack since he was their only child. He explained that their home was in a small town of about 3,200. He went on to tell me that Jack was a good son, that he always brought his friends and girlfriends home to meet his parents and that his former classmates still made a point of stopping by to visit.

Almost every day I think about my lost friend and use his image to inspire me, to help me overcome the physical and emotional scars of Vietnam. It is partly my memories of Jack that help me strive to better myself and to encourage and respect others, human traits that we all should practice. I hope that someday, boys like Jack, myself, and many other young Americans will never be ripped from their wombs of home to fight a senseless war like the one in Vietnam.

Distinguished Service Cross Award

After having reviewed the Distinguished Service Cross Award post on 3/31/2021 and other reports, I determined that Jack must have picked up the grenade and was throwing it when he looked back at me and smiled.

I was busy at the time firing at the enemy and dealing with a bullet that went through my right biceps, so I didn't see where he got the grenade. I always assumed it was one of his. Now, I believe he must have picked up the grenade and it must have gone off just after he threw it, since his left side was injured.

Robert M. Braun, Sr.

I was on his right side and he threw it with his right hand. It must have been in the air, or in his hand, when it went off. The enemy was in front of us on our left side.

This saved my life, because Jack absorbed most of the shrapnel from the grenade. I have relived this many, many times over the years; I now have a clearer picture of what happened. This has only motivated me more to keep Jack's story alive.

The following two chapters **"First Last Rites"** and **"Second Last Rites"** are what I remember during the moments when I regained consciousness after fighting for my life. Over the following weeks I was either unconscious or blinded from my head injury and from the Grand Mal Seizure I had when I was being flown to Japan.

The final chapter is entitled, **"Going Home"**.

Robert M. Braun, Sr.

First Last Rites

The date was March 31st, 1970. I had just been injured in a firefight and the following are events that happened in the weeks and months that eventually led to going home.

After the medic told me that I had all my body parts, I went out again. The next time I regained consciousness, I was being carried by one of the Spanish speaking new members of our unit, over his shoulder. This is when I had an out-of-body experience. I remember seeing everything in black and white and was about twenty to thirty feet above the ground. This is when I saw my buddy Jack's body being recovered. It still brings tears whenever I relive the event.

The next thing I remember is being carried into a B-52 bomb crater. I am not sure how long it took for the Dust-off helicopter to arrive but I do remember being laid down onto the floor of the helicopter, and giving a thumbs up sign to some of the other guys in my unit before throwing up as the chopper took off.

A CASEVAC is a casualty evacuation, call sign Dust off, of a patient evacuation of casualties from a combat zone. The Casevac can be done by ground or air and were almost all done by helicopter in Vietnam.

The difference between a MEDEVAC (medical evacuation) and the CASEVAC is that the Casevac is used to transport casualties from the battlefield that are in dire need of evacuation and don't have time to wait for a Medevac. Casevac or Dust off helicopters are allowed to be armed because they are used for other purposes. Medevac helicopters are clearly marked with a red cross and it is a war crime under Article II of the Geneva Convention if fired upon while evacuating injured soldiers.

Another primary difference is, the Casevac uses non-dedicated vehicles that may or may not provide care along the way for the injured soldiers and are, lift/flight of opportunity meaning, the closest available unit provides transportation to the nearest medical hospital. Ref.35

I was unconscious throughout the ride to the 12th Evacuation Hospital in Cu Chi, the Headquarters of the 25th Infantry, and didn't regain consciousness until I screamed, "you're putting a tree in me," and felt hands grabbing my arms to hold me down. They were putting a foley catheter in me since I had a groin injury, and to prepare me for the upcoming neurosurgery.

The 12th Evacuation Hospital mission, and other American division hospitals, are there to provide hospitalization to all classes of patients in the combat zones. It is the same place Jack and I were flown to when we were injured on January 21st, 1970.

The personnel at the hospitals performed extensive medical and surgical operations and procedures on outpatients and extensive emergency medical treatment to injured soldiers.

In my case the first thing that had to be done was to stop the bleeding since I had a number of injuries, the worst was the head. After being held down, I was anesthetized for the neurosurgery which included a craniectomy, and am not sure how long I was in surgery, or the length of time I was unconscious.

A craniectomy includes the removal of a bone flap, but in my case, it is not returned to its location after the procedure is finished. This may be because the bone itself is too damaged, the brain is too swollen to reattach the flap, or the surgeon feels it is in the patient's best interest not to replace it. Ref. 36

I can remember awakening, unable to see anything, but I could tell I had intravenous catheters in both arms and restraints on both my arms and legs. My head was bandaged, and I could feel work had been done to the right side of my head just behind the right ear.

My very first thought was: there was, **NO WAY** I was going out in the field again. I knew that injured soldiers do return to the field. One of my platoon members, former point man Pusher, returned after he was wounded. I also knew that if you were injured enough, you would be sent home. The other point man, from Washington State, and the member of my unit that was injured by a Claymore Mine, when on top of Black Virgin Mountain, were injured badly enough that their tour was over. I thought I would have gone to LBJ, if my injuries were not bad enough to be sent home. There was **NO WAY**, I was going back out into the jungles to fight again.

LBJ (Long Binh Jail) was located at Long Binh Post, about 20 kilometers northeast of Saigon and was a stockade of the U.S. military during the Vietnam War. In 1966 the jail was established and designed as a temporary stockade to hold about four hundred prisoners, and at times housed over seven hundred inmates.

The prisoners were separated into minimum, medium, and maximum security. A five by seven-foot sheet metal and wood box, or a Conex Container, that measured six by nine feet, housed individual maximum-security prisoners. Other areas included a mess hall, work area, cells for other prisoners, and an administrative building. Ref. 37

It was known to be a real bad place, but would have been a whole lot better than stomping through the jungle, searching for Charlie, carrying one-hundred pounds or more of equipment, in a hundred plus degree heat, with potential death around every turn. It was my biggest worry after regaining consciousness. There was **No Way**, I was going back into the field!

Once a nurse saw I was awake, she welcomed me back to the world again and told me I had been out for a little over a week: that I had a serious brain operation. She went on to tell me I was lucky and had the last rites when I was returned from the field to the 12th Evacuation Hospital in Cu Chi; my **First Last Rites**.

I didn't stay conscious very long but long enough to think about some of the missions I had been on and telling myself there was **No Way**, I would go out to fight, again.

One of my first thoughts was about an early mission on my tour when I was still carrying the M-79 Grenade Launcher. We had been flown into a Hot LZ while a few VC were having their breakfast. I was on the right side of the helicopter near the door ready to jump out, the side gunner of the chopper was shooting into the hedgerow; shells flying everywhere. Smoke could be seen coming out of the hedgerow.

Once out, the squad lined up and moved towards a creek that ran along the field where we landed. Many, many times I asked myself and questioned how I would react when we moved in a line towards our enemy. Would I move forwardly as a unit as I was trained in Basic and Advanced Infantry Training? I did as I was trained. As we moved towards the creek, a VC was spotted running in it.

My M-79 was loaded with a high explosive round and I fired at the trees hoping the high explosive round's shrapnel would hit the VC. When we got to the creek it took a right turn. Jack, and another guy in our unit went into the creek following the VC, one guy walked on the left side, and I walked down the right. A helicopter flew low just in front of us.

I had changed to a shotgun round for my M-79 and we all moved down the creek. I had never killed a human before but if I had to, I would. After we moved down the creek a little, the chopper flying just above the treetops opened fire with their left side machine-gun, then dropped off a smoke grenade. We moved up to the smoke and saw a VC lying in the creek with holes over most of his body; he was dead. It was one VC that didn't eat that breakfast, or any other.

The second mission I thought about, was when my unit was moving to our next ambush. I had been in country for about three months. Jack was in the lead and I followed closely behind. As we walked down a trail it started to smell really badly. It got so bad we had to cover our noses with one of our hands. A short way up the trail we ran into a couple of dead VCs. They had been dead for a few days, their skin was turning into leather from the hot sun, and boy did they smell.

One of the bodies was ripped apart with legs and lower parts of the body, from the waist down, on one side of the trail and the rest of his body on the other. What bothered me the most was, it didn't matter to me that two men were killed. I was getting hardened by the killing I had seen; I was becoming insensitive to it. I was taught when growing up that; "Thou Shalt Not Kill".

The chance of heading back out into the field haunted me. When I recovered somewhat, I asked the nurse taking care of me if I would be sent out again when I recovered. She told me with my head injury I was lucky to be alive. (Only fourteen percent of head injuries in Vietnam survived.) I can still remember the relief I felt, like a huge weight was lifted from my shoulders, knowing I would not be sent back out and that I would be heading home. First, I would have to recover before being sent to Japan, then home. I was going home. I would make it back to my twin's wedding to be his best man, like I promised before I left for Vietnam. I was going home. **I was, going, home!**

The next few days I began to regain my strength, my eyesight, and remained awake for short periods of time. For the next week or so I remained awake a little longer, enough to have visitors. I still had intravenous catheters, the restraints on both my arms and legs: head, back, groin, right arm and leg were still bandaged.

A Roman Catholic priest came to my bedside to bless me and say a few prayers. I was not able to receive communion since I was not taking anything by mouth yet, still had intravenous catheters in both arms, bandages around my head, and on my other injuries. The restraints on both my arms and legs had finally been removed.

One of the nurses told me I had pieces of metal in my back and one piece penetrated into my head on the right side just behind the right ear. Part of my skull had been removed; that because of the injury my brain was swollen causing the partial blindness. She said I would regain eyesight in time.

Around the fourteenth of April, Lieutenant Sparks came to visit me. He was heading back out to our unit in the field and had recovered from the shrapnel wounds he received on the thirty-first. I was scheduled to be flown to Japan in the next few days.

We had talked about the space program while we were out in the field. I had told Jack, Lieutenant Sparks, and a few of the other guys, that I followed it, saw Neil Armstrong walk on the moon while in Basic Training, and saw Neil at The Bob Hope Christmas Show.

Lieutenant Sparks and I had already talked about Jack on an earlier short visit, that he didn't make it, and his body was already sent home. We both said a few prayers for his soul.

Since we had talked about the space program, Lieutenant Sparks wanted to take me to hear the news about Apollo 13. It was launched on April eleventh and had an explosion on its way to the moon on the second day of the flight, the thirteenth of April. He had gotten a wheelchair and helped me out of the bed and into the wheelchair. As he was wheeling me to the rec room I started feeling lightheaded and everything was unfocused.

When we finally got in front of the TV, I told Lieutenant Sparks I couldn't see anything and that I didn't feel well. He had to return me to my bed and I was unconscious by the time we got there. It was an aura that normally occurs just before the beginning of a seizure.

Robert M. Braun, Sr.

Second Last Rites

The next thing I remember, I was strapped down in bed again with the intravenous catheters still in both arms and had no idea what had happened nor how long I was out. When I regained consciousness for a few moments a nurse was at my side. This is when I found out that I had a grand mal seizure when I was being sent to the Tan Son Nhut Airport, to be flown to Japan. They had to VIP me, via helicopter, back to the hospital in Cu Chi and that is when I had my **Second Last Rites**. They were not sure I was going to make it.

The doctors placed me into a medically induced coma. On April 24, 1970, a Friday, I was sent to Japan. I know it was the 24th since I was in Vietnam for four months and eleven days. I arrived in Vietnam on December 13, 1969.

I was unconscious for the entire trip to the airport and for most of the flight to Japan but remember regaining consciousness for a brief moment and remember seeing other injured soldiers lying on gurneys around the plane. During the flight I was strapped down with intravenous catheters in both arms and a foley catheter. The gears and wires on the jet were all visible. On the gurney across from me was what looked like a hunk of meat. The only way I knew it was a human was I heard it moaning. It took me a while to realize that the guy must have been burned over most of his body; I cannot imagine the pain and suffering he must have felt.

The next thing I remember is being laid down in a bed in the Neurology Ward of the hospital in Japan. The bandages were on my head, back, groin, right arm, leg, and all the tubes were still in me. In the bed across from me was a guy that really looked messed up. His head was bandaged, cardiac electrodes and monitoring devices in place, right arm elevated and in a cast with an opening near the elbow for a wound that needed to be treated, right leg was wrapped in bandages, intravenous catheters in both arms, oxygen mask in place, and was strapped to the bed. He must have been in pain because he groaned a lot.

Neurology from Greek: vevpov (neuron), "string, nerve" and the suffix-logia "study of", is a branch of medicine dealing with disorders of the nervous system. Neurology deals with the diagnosis and treatment of all categories of conditions and diseases involving the brain, the spinal cord, and the peripheral nerves. Neurological practice relies heavily on the field of neuroscience, the scientific study of the nervous system. Ref.38

A nurse taking care of us told me that he had been injured by a grenade booby trap and had a head injury, much like mine, but worse: his right arm was broken, and his right leg from the knee down had been injured badly by shrapnel from the grenade. Looking at him made me realize how lucky I was, my injuries could have been a lot worse; provided me with the inspiration to fight hard to recover.

A few days later, the world was coming back. I was regaining consciousness for short periods, and asked the nurse if she could start taking my temperature in my mouth instead of my rectum. She got the OK. I was on my way to recovery. While awake, I watched the guy across from me recuperate as well. First his oxygen mask, then the cardiac electrodes and monitoring devices were disconnected, and his moaning decreased.

After I continued to improve, my restraints were removed and I was getting out of bed for short periods of time and beginning to eat by mouth. I still had my head, back, groin, leg, and right bicep bandaged, one intravenous catheter for intravenous antibiotics, and the foley catheter. When out of bed and moving, I had to carry the foley bag and pull the intravenous pole, with the intravenous fluids and antibiotics hanging on the pole above heart level.

Walking around the Neurology Ward, the physical consequences of war, were demonstrated.

A guy that I would talk to and feed was paralyzed from the neck down, a quadriplegic. Another man was paralyzed from the waist down, a paraplegic. One had a large piece of metal hit the frontal lobe of his brain and would be a vegetable for the rest of his life. We all would suffer Post Traumatic Stress Disorder (PTSD) for the rest of our lives while living with our injuries.

Although most veterans were not permanently damaged by the war, some 15 to 25 percent of Vietnam veterans (between 500,000 and 700,000) suffered from a stress-related impairment known as post-traumatic stress disorder (PTSD), a psychological disease brought on by acute combat experience. Some of the 11,500 women who served in the war—90 percent of them as nurses—also returned exhibiting PTSD. This condition can occur in combat soldiers or other individuals suffering from violent trauma and can manifest itself years after the initial experience. Also known as shell shock or combat fatigue disorder.

For confidential support, *vets and loved ones can contact the Veterans Crisis Line at 800-273-8255 or text 838255.* Ref. 39

The soldier that was a quadriplegic told me, while I fed him, that he was from South Carolina, used to play a guitar in a band before being drafted into the Army, and knew he would never play again. I encouraged him to not give up but use the most important asset he had, his mind. He could still talk and maybe he could start composing music.

While helping the nurses by feeding and just talking to my fellow wounded soldiers, my war brothers, I would always encourage them to fight to get better, tell them every day we move closer to going home, and we all had survived Vietnam. Listening to my own advice, I worked hard to improve, knowing the faster I healed, the sooner I would be going home to be with my family and friends. **We were all going home!**

The shrapnel in my back were in too deep to be removed, and the wounds were opened, debrided, drained, flushed, and bandaged daily. The bullet wound in my right bicep was bandaged and healing. I was fortunate that the bullet passed through my muscle and did not fracture the bone. I was also fortunate that none of the shrapnel severed my backbone and/or my spinal cord; a number of pieces were really close. If just one piece had hit my backbone and/or my spinal cord, I may have been quadriplegic like my friend from South Carolina, or a paraplegic.

The wounds in my back ended up getting infected because I was spending so much time away from my bed helping other injured men, and not enough time in my own bed to have my injuries treated. A nurse had to inject antibiotics into the wounds to clear up the infections and reprimanded me for not taking care of myself. I told her, I just wanted to help the guys that were worse off than me. She gave me a smile, and said, "I understand but you need to take better care of yourself". I did as I was told.

One day the Neurology Ward was visited by a four-piece country music band. The female singer, I will call Jane, was really pretty with long blond hair, great figure, round eyes, and had a beautiful voice. My friend in the bed across from me really liked the band and especially the girl singer, Jane. After the band left, I asked him if he enjoyed the music and if he liked her. He nodded his head yes and I told him I would try to go get Jane for him. He gave me the biggest smile.

After asking the nurse if it was OK, carrying the foley bag and pulling the intravenous pole, I went out into the hallway, outside the Neurology Ward where the band was standing and asked Jane if she would come visit my friend, because he really liked her, and she happily agreed. When we reached my friend, he was sitting up in his bed, maybe for the first time with the biggest smile. He had trouble talking, but she was great, giving him a big kiss on the cheek before she left. He couldn't have been happier, and so was I. All the nurses saw this, thanked me, and gave me big hugs.

We both continued to improve. Finally, the day came when my foley catheter was going to be removed. It was taken out early in the day, and boy was I happy to be free again.

New patients came steadily into the Neurology Ward, while others there before me, were well enough to be sent home. My South Carolina friend, who used to play the guitar, was sent home along with the soldier who was a paraplegic. I made sure I said my goodbyes, and wished them the best of luck back in the states.

My across the aisle friend was still in his bed. I visited him, like I did every day. This time I was without the foley bag. For the rest of the day, I visited some of the newly injured men in the Neurology Ward.

There was one young soldier that was a casualty of a Claymore Mine. He had no left arm, no legs from the knees down, a head injury, and a real big heart. Every time I visited him he told me he was doing OK and thanked me for asking. His Claymore Mine injuries were far worse than the accident that happened to a member of my unit when on top of Black Virgin Mountain.

It amazed me that the human body could suffer so much damage and still continue to live. Seeing all the suffering made me appreciate the will to survive and, the **beauty of life**. I went to bed that night happy I was free of all the tubes in me and knowing I was closer to going home, maybe in the next few days.

Thoughts of getting close to going home had me thinking of my sisters, brothers, mother, father, grandparents, all my friends, and my family.

The oldest girl, Barbara, had just turned twenty, graduated the same year, 1968, with my twin and I. She was working for the State of New Jersey and was dating her high school sweetheart.

Next came Kathy; she was a High School cheerleader and was in her senior year in High School. She was dating one of my best friends. He was the one who had the car we used to cruise around the backroads. Barbara and Kathy were both cheerleaders for our midget football team. This made up the first half of the family; five of us in three and a half years. The second half of the family was made up of three girls and one boy.

The Family

The oldest of the second half was Maryann and next was Margaret. They just started school in Trenton after my parents sold the house where I grew up, and moved to the home my mother inherited from her mother. They had to live there until a new home was built in Titusville, New Jersey, not far from our old home in Washington Crossing.

The youngest boy Carl, the eighth member of the family, the one who stood up to the bully in his new school, was now ten. The baby of the family was Carrie, now eight, helped make the chocolate chip cookies that all my buddies enjoyed in the package I had received while out in the field.

It was a large family and we were all close. Whenever there was a party, Barbara and Kathy knew they would be safe because their big brothers were there. We all stuck together.

Steve, the oldest, was drafted by the Minnesota Twins in 1967 after he graduated from high school and was away at spring training. My twin brother, Rich, was working as a draftsman and selling his art. He was getting married in July and I would be home in time to be his best man.

Then there was our closest friend Richie, who was dating Kathy. He was the one that threw the coming home party for my older brother and the going away party for me. My older brother was getting out of the Army and I had just begun Basic Training. Richie always had cool cars like the 1957 Chevy he had throughout high school. We all watched the introduction of the Beatles on the Ed Sullivan Show, in his bedroom. He was also the one who rode on my twin brother's and my shoulders in the Fourth of July Boat Show, along with being the friend that drove to Sarasota, Florida with my twin and I for my brother's second year in the Minor Leagues. Many nights my brothers and I stayed at his place after a party.

The past six months were the longest I had been away from my family and friends. I went to sleep that night with a smile knowing I would be seeing them soon.

Back at home.
My family knew I had been hurt. I later found out a letter had been delivered to my home informing my family of my injuries. The person who was home when the letter arrived, just happened to be, my twin brother Rich. When the rest of the family got home my twin was sitting in one of my grandmother's rocking chairs, in SHOCK! He handed the letter to my father. After reading the letter, my father dropped to the floor, unable to believe that there was a question if I would live and if I did, would I be alright. My father gathered all the family and went to church to say prayers for me. I also found out later, that after walking back from the gate at the John F. Kennedy Airport in New York City, I was on the plane on my way to Oakland, California, then Vietnam, my father turned to my older brother, Steve, and told him he thought this maybe the last time the family would ever see me alive, again.

Every day they watched the news on TV, the body count, the fighting in Vietnam, and watched The Bob Hope Christmas Show looking for me, like so many other families that had children, a brother or a sister, relatives, or friends serving in Vietnam. I had already written telling them that I guarded the stage for The Bob Hope Christmas Show, went to it, and was not wearing a shirt, so they knew I was at the show. I received a letter a few weeks later telling me, that the whole family gathered around the TV and looked for me, but couldn't find me because almost all the guys, were not wearing shirts.

I sent home my first Purple Heart after receiving it at the Stand Down after my twenty-first birthday, from the injuries received on January 21, 1970. I had already told them about my best friend Jack Smith, that we were walking point together, and that he was a lot like my twin brother Rich. I knew they missed me. It was so, so hard to be away from them.

Back to my fight to return home.

That night I had a good night, sleeping for the first time in over four weeks without anything in me, just bandages on my head, right leg, arm, and back. I woke up early the next morning thinking I may receive news that I would be going home in the next few days. That, did, not, happen!

Instead, I woke up thinking I must have had an accident during the night because the bottom of my Army issued pajamas were wet. I hadn't wet my bed since I was very young. Something, was wrong.

When I looked to check my pajama bottoms, they had changed from light blue to red. My groin injury had opened up and bled during the night. Boy, was it depressing. Now, I knew I wasn't going home in the next few days.

I called the nurse and showed her what had happened. Blood was still dripping from my groin injury, so she got some bandages and I sat on the edge of my bed applying pressure to my injury to stop the bleeding. The nurse had to call a specialist, a Urologist, to reinsert, over a glidewire, a two-way coude tip silicone foley catheter, after applying a generous amount of topical xylocaine jelly. Vaseline coated gauze pressure bandages, telfa, and sterile 4"x4" gauze dressings were then applied to my urethra to stop the hemorrhaging. I lost so much blood that blood transfusions were administered over the next several hours.

It took a while for the doctor to arrive. During the wait, I sat naked from the waist down applying pressure. I didn't care who saw me. I was so down knowing my going home would be delayed for another week or two, maybe longer. But, knowing and seeing so many other men in far worse shape than me helped to overcome this setback. I knew I would eventually heal and would be going home, walking, and talking, NOT like so many others I had helped and all the others that were severely injured while serving in Vietnam.

After having the coude silicone foley catheter inserted, and after the blood transfusions were completed, I was carrying the foley bag around again. I went to see my friend and told him what had happened. He just shook his head and tried to say he was sorry. I understood what he was trying to say and thanked him. He was much improved and he was starting to eat a soft diet by mouth. He had to eat with his left arm because his right was still broken and in a cast, but the wound on his arm was much better.

For the next few days, I was in a great deal of pain from the Vaseline coated gauze pressure bandages. They had to be tight to stop the bleeding. I still tried to help every day but had to spend more time in bed. Helping did take my mind off the pain. Each day a nurse had to check the catheter frequently to make sure I was not hemorrhaging. The nurse also redressed my other wounds.

While spending more time in bed thoughts of home dominated my thinking. Across the Delaware River from Washington Crossing, New Jersey, are the same buildings that were there during the Revolutionary War. I saw them every day. They were just down the street from my home. Sometimes, I would stand looking at them and thought that I was looking at the same thing as George Washington would have seen in 1776.

I missed the sunsets on the river: how the colors were painted across the sky, the excitement of catching a nice Small Mouth Bass, the thrill of water skiing up and down the river, floating down the Delaware on inner tubes with my brothers, sisters, and friends. All helped me overcome the challenges of surviving the harsh country of Vietnam and overcome this setback.

I had received a letter from my friend Richie. He wrote me that the new dock on the river right down from his home was almost done.

One weekend in August when I was home, just shot expert on the rifle range to earn the weekend pass, he drove his boat down the river in front of his parent's home where we wanted the dock to be built. I jumped into the river to make sure it was deep enough. It ended up being a perfect place for the dock and was the only one on the New Jersey side south of the Washington Crossing Bridge and north of Trenton.

Robert M. Braun, Sr.

In between the dock and his parent's home was Route 29, a steep bank, the Delaware Raritan Canal, train tracks, and a real steep bank to the river. There was nothing that could have been done with the road. You just had to be careful crossing it. Steps were built for both steep banks of the canal and river, and a small barge was attached to a cable, and ski ropes attached to the bank were used to pull the barge across the canal. A large deck was built on the bank of the river and a fireplace for cooking was added. I couldn't wait to get back to check out the new dock.

The Delaware Raritan Canal was built in the 1830s to connect the Raritan River with the Delaware River to transport freight between Philadelphia and New York City. Coal from anthracite fields in eastern Pennsylvania during the 19th and early 20th centuries was the major merchandise shipped.

William Penn suggested the canal back in the 1690s, and in 1816 New Jersey created a commission of three individuals including John Rutherfurd a former U.S. Senator. New Jersey passed legislation creating a charter to build the canal on February 4, 1830. Work began later in 1830, dug mostly by Irish immigrants by hand and was completed in 1834. Teams of mules were used to pull the boats up and down the canal on a tow path. Ref. 40

Today the canal is a park with a towpath along it which was once used for railroad tracks. In 1974 it was declared a New Jersey State Park and is used for canoeing, kayaking, and fishing. The towpath is perfect for bike riding and jogging. The canal was a great place to fish. I fished it many times growing up, and still fish it today.

These thoughts helped me suppress the loss of my really good friend Jack. I knew that smile he gave me would be with me the rest of my life along with seeing his body being recovered. What has helped to lessen the pain of his loss over the years, was remembering the great, good times we had when we were together. We were closer than brothers. We were like twins.

Some of my most cherished memories include: thoughts about the first day meeting my unit, Jack was right there. He saw my hometown of Titusville and said you live in "tit us ville". We all got a good laugh. That big smile he gave me when I had to turn over my

M-16 to him and got the M-79 in exchange, spending time recovering from our first injuries in Cu Chi, the great meals we had in the Officers Mess Hall, the massages we got from pretty Vietnamese girls, how we practiced shooting baskets and played a little one on one, the time on a Stand Down when our team kicked butt in basketball games, when we both received our Purple Hearts, the two weeks we spent on top of Black Virgin Mountain, swimming in the Saigon River, and the leeches at the waterhole; all are my most treasured memories of Jack. I carry them today, and will carry them for the rest of my life. All these memories have inspired me to write, and always do the best I can while enjoying the **Beauty of Life**.

We had talked about college. I decided to attend college on my twenty-first birthday while in a firefight. Jack said he would go back for his sophomore year. We both knew we each wanted a family, because we both loved young kids so much, and wanted to make sure we could afford one. It was a dream we both shared.

Over the past month or so I noticed that Jack was looking into the future more. When we first became friends, he didn't talk about the future or his past very much. As we got closer, he opened up a little. He had gotten a couple of letters from his high school sweetheart that seemed to pick him up.

The goal of going to college and having a family, didn't and will never happen for Jack but, I did fulfill our dream, and promise, with the help of memories of him. I ended up graduating from Rider University in 1977 and enjoy a family of three children: Kimberly, Robert, and Emily, as well as two grandchildren, Andrew, and Jenna.

Over the next three or four days the pain let up and my wounds were healing. My friend continued to improve. His talking was getting better and he was starting to eat solid meals. I kept telling him that every day we were getting closer to going home.

Finally, after a week, the nurse thought that my groin injury was healed enough to have the coude silicone foley catheter removed. The Urologist was called to remove the catheter. After the catheter was removed the wound on my urethra was much better with a large scab on the injury. The nurse bandaged it to protect it from opening up again. The first thing I did was go into the bathroom to urinate standing up. It was so, so nice to be close to normal. Now that I was over my setback, I began to get ready to go home.

My friend was also much improved. He was sitting up in bed and his talking was getting better. It was doubtful he would ever completely recover and be able to talk clearly again. His head injury was much more serious than mine and would affect his ability to live a normal life without care.

I was doing great, walking around the Neurology Ward visiting and talking to the newly injured soldiers that had just arrived from Vietnam. I was doing as much as I could to help the nurses. Another thing I was doing was getting my Army dress uniform, to be ready to be flown home. I still had bandages on all my wounds but I was determined to go home, in style.

A day before I was scheduled to return home, my friend was on his way home. We said our goodbyes and wished each other good luck.

After he was gone a nurse came to me and told me that my friend was going home early because I had spent so much time with him helping and encouraging him to fight to get better. She gave me a big hug and thanked me. A few other nurses thanked me as well.

I was in a hospital somewhere near Tokyo and would be flying out early the next morning along with other injured soldiers well enough to be flown back to the states. I went to bed that night, feeling both happy and relieved, knowing I was going home. My dress uniform was hanging near my bed along with my newly issued Army fatigues. I was, **GOING, HOME**.

It would be a long flight, almost seven thousand miles with a layover in Alaska for refueling, then on to Andrews Air Force Base in Washington D. C. and Walter Reed Hospital. I was told by a Neurosurgeon that I would have to wait at least a year before an amalgamate plate would be inserted in the hole where the skull had to be removed. That is the reason why I was being sent to Walter Reed Hospital; it was where the Neurosurgery would take place to insert the plate.

While in bed that night I tried to remember the names of the men with whom I served. The only full names I could remember were Jack Rae Smith and Lieutenant Kenneth Sparks. It is one of my biggest regrets. My head injury may have caused part of my Vietnam memories to be permanently destroyed and may be one of the reasons why, I cannot recall the full real names of the members of my unit.

Many of these stories are based on what I do remember and on the many letters I sent home. My Mother saved them for me along with a few pictures I took while serving in Vietnam.

Getting Jack's 1967 High School yearbook and information from Jack's friends, Scott Case, Dennis Hoffman, Craig Bergstrom helped me recall many of the things Jack and I talked about, along with many of the things, we may have talked about. We spent every day for almost four months together working as a team, mostly on our own, living with the threat of potential death every day.

VIETNAM MEMORIAL
Is located in Washington, D. C. is a national memorial honoring service members who died or remain missing while serving in the Vietnam War.

Robert M. Braun, Sr.

Going Home

During the day I visited the injured men in the **Neurology Ward** for the last time, wishing them luck and telling them not to stop fighting to get better. After having my last meal in a faraway country, I settled in my hospital bed planning to get a good night sleep for the big day tomorrow. I was going home. I was finally, going, home.

While lying in bed thoughts drifted back to when I was around nine and it was an early summer day. We had gotten the yard ready for the family picnic. The tablecloths were on the picnic tables. This was the first family picnic of the year. A few of my uncles and cousins were coming, along with some of the kids in the neighborhood, **and my grandparents**.

Our backyard was the playground for the kids that lived around us, and there was always someone ready to play. At night we played hide and go seek, cops and robbers, tag, Cowboys and Indians, played basketball games or shot baskets on our lighted court. Sometimes we played a card game called Catch Five. It was a pretty easy game to play. This was another place my twin and I seldom lost. We had a way to communicate nonverbally. Even early in our life we were able to know what the other was thinking. We won so much the other kids complained, and we were not allowed to play as a team.

We had a big backyard with a swing set and a tire swing hanging from a large branch on a huge tree that was near the basketball court with a ten-foot basket. In between the huge tree and the basketball court was a quoit pit where we played quoits when not shooting baskets. Both the yard and neighborhood were a great place to play for all the kids.

My grandparents arrived early, bringing the hot dogs and hamburgers, buns, rolls, potato chips, and soda. My Mother made a big batch of potato salad, baked beans, and cucumber salad. When my uncles and cousins arrived, the fire was started and the cooking began. After everyone had eaten the cards came out. My

Grandfather and Father teamed up; they were known to be good card players and my twin and I played them in Catch Five.

The rules of Catch Five are: thirteen cards are dealt out to each player and there are nine points possible in each hand. The points are added up for each hand and the first to twenty-one wins. If a nine and out is called and is made, the game is over. Each player bids how many points the team can make and the highest bidder calls the suit. You had to play the suit in your hand if you had one.

The points are: high, low, jack, and ten of the suit called, are worth one point, and five of the suit is worth five points, for a total of nine. My Grandfather dealt first. I was sitting across the table from him, my Father was to the left of me, and my twin sat across from me on the other side of the picnic table, next to my Grandfather.

My Grandfather dealt the cards out, and I picked up my cards and saw an ace, king, queen, ten, and nine of clubs, a really good hand. I was the first to bid so my Grandfather looked at me to make my bid. Looking down at my cards, I bid nine and out. My Grandfather and Father looked at me with a look of shock. I ended up making my nine and out and my twin and I won the game.

It was my turn to deal for the second game. I dealt out all of the cards. My Father made a low bid and my twin Rich said, "Nine and out." Our opponents were shocked, again. Rich made hearts the suit and he made his nine and out also. That was enough for our Grandfather and Father. They got up from the table shaking their heads and said, "You guys have some kind of secret communication or something!"

This is part of an article about twin communication from Psychology Today, August 30, 2021.

An Insider's Perspective: How Twins Communicate

Twins are born communicators. Even before very young twins learn language, they can and will communicate nonverbally by looking at each other, staying close together, or hitting each other—and of course playing with each other.

More often than not, twins have a special language that parents and relatives don't understand without a great deal of effort. Ref. 41

This was when my twin and I were nine years old; we had a way to connect without words. We were separated at the beginning of fifth grade, when we were sent to different schools because our fourth-grade teacher complained that the two of us dominated the classroom. If anyone picked on one, they ended up dealing with two.

I continued, unknowingly, to use this innate skill because I was not with my twin. I became a one-on-one kind of individual. It may be one of the many reasons why Jack and I became best friends. Jack was the quarterback in football, point guard of his basketball teams, and co-captain for both. He had to develop communication skills to be the great athlete and team player he became. We were able to use nonverbal communication to know and understand each other, just like my twin and I. It may be part of the reasons why, along with my head injury, I am unable to remember the full/real names of the other men with whom I served.

Another memory that flashed into my head was when I again used twin communication to know something was wrong with my twin. It was on a Saturday night after I played my trumpet at a sock hop, with a few other members of our high school band. I was lead trumpet and got to play two songs that I played every day.

One of the songs that the band played was "When the Saints Go Marching In". It was one of the songs I practiced every day to warm up my lips. I just enjoyed playing it and had watched Louis Armstrong and his band perform many times. Another song I practiced every day was "Moon River".

My family got tired of hearing many of the songs I played because I played them every day. I would go into the bedroom shared with my three brothers and practice. In eighth grade, in shop class, I made a real cool wooden music stand and kept my music on it, always ready. Some of the songs I played, like the two above, I could play from memory.

Our little band, played a number of other songs that the other students at the sock hop could dance to, that included some of the popular songs of the time. It was a lot of fun and I went home feeling pretty good.

My twin, Rich, hadn't gotten home yet. He had gone to a party instead of the sock hop. I was lying in bed, couldn't sleep, and had a bad feeling that something was wrong with Rich. I guess it was **twin communication**.

The phone rang. I jumped from the top bunk and beat everyone to the phone, even though I was the furthest from it. I knew something was wrong. Sure enough, the call was to tell us Rich was in the hospital and had been in an auto accident. He was hurt badly, had a bad concussion, broken ribs, and punctured lung.

After spending most of the night and next day at the hospital, I went to look at the car. Rich had been in the passenger seat, the death seat. It was amazing Rich survived. The dashboard was dented in and the windshield had a big hole where Rich's head had hit. He had a **Traumatic Brain Injury.**

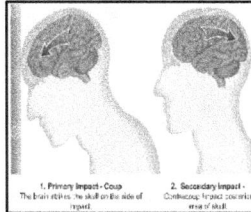

DREAMSTIME.com

Traumatic Brain Injury is one of the causes of Dementia/Alzheimer. The brain is rocked back and forth inside the skull causing damage. The medical term is *contrecoup*.

Official explanation of TBI:

Traumatic Brain Injury (TBI) is sudden damage to the brain caused by a blow or jolt to the head. Common causes include car or motorcycle crashes, falls, sports injuries, and assaults. Injuries can range from mild concussions to severe permanent brain damage. While treatment for mild TBI may include rest and medication, severe TBI may require intensive care and life-saving surgery. Those who survive a brain injury can face lasting effects in their physical and mental abilities, as well as emotions and personality. Most people who suffer moderate to severe TBI will need rehabilitation to recover and relearn skills. Ref. 42

Traumatic Brain Injury is believed to have been the cause, why Rich suffered with Dementia that eventually took his life. My twin brother left this world on November 26, 2013 and was only sixty-four years old.

Taking care of him was harder than surviving the jungles of Vietnam. I watched him go from a strong healthy man to a helpless individual that weighed less than one hundred pounds. The hardships I witnessed in Vietnam helped me overcome the loss of both my twin brother Rich and good friend Jack. Their loss continues to inspire me to push forward in performing my moral duty to help point out injustices and untruths. See five articles, that were published in local papers in the chapter: **"Make My Point that War and Violence are Not the Answer"**.

Back to going home.

I was scheduled to leave real early the next morning, the second week in May 1970. All those that were well enough were to meet the C-9A at the airport by 0600 hours. The hospital that had been my home for the last three weeks or so was somewhere near Tokyo, Japan, and it would take about forty-five minutes to get to the airport, not sure what airport.

Rising early, I began to get ready. My dress uniform was hanging at my bedside. I was proud to be heading home in style. It would be the first time in full dress uniform since back in the states.

On the right shoulder was the blue braid of the Army Infantry. On the left side of the Army dress uniform were the Vietnam Service Ribbons, along with the Combat Infantry Medal. On the left shoulder was the 25th Infantry Division Patch.

A nurse had come by after I got up, to redress my wounds. After she was done, I got dressed; ready to go. Boy did it feel good knowing that by the end of the day I would be back in the USA.

At around 0430 hours I was on my way home. As I walked to the bus my rank was PFC Private First Class. I knew how to play the Army part but I always considered myself a civilian. Being drafted, my time in the service was for only two long years.

I was proud to have served my Country, helped the nurses, encouraged other injured men to strive to get better, was pleased that I was able to get the country girl singer for my friend, and knew I did as much as possible to survive and to help others. I was ready, to go home.

An Army olive green bus with Red Cross markings on it was waiting. There were a few other veterans well enough to travel home. We were all lucky to have survived Vietnam but, we would all return different men than when we arrived in this war torn country.

It was still dark when the bus took off so I was not able to see anything of Tokyo or where I was in Japan. It took maybe forty-five minutes to get to the airport. There waiting for us was the C-9A, the U.S. Air Force's first specially designed aeromedical evacuation aircraft.

The C-9A debuted in August 1968 and was the answer to the demand for a more effective way to transport patients from the Vietnam War. It was known as the "Cadillac of Medevac" by the pilots that flew it, and the medical staff that cared for the injured men. The C-9A had two twin jet engines, and could carry up to forty patients, both ambulatory and those on stretchers.

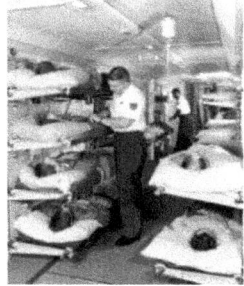

The C-9A was essentially a flying hospital. I was one of a handful of patients that were able to walk onto the C-9A and took a seat on the right side of the jet. Looking out the window, I could see other Vietnam warriors that could not walk, carried on stretchers, onto the plane. Some were without arms or legs, while others were like me, with bandages around their heads. Looking at them again made me appreciate how lucky I was. Ref. 46

The C-9A took off on time. I was heading home, glued to the window watching every mile as I moved closer to be with my family. I knew I would have to spend more time in the Army to serve my two years but, not in a country that I just bearly survived and Jack and many others did not.

It took about fourteen hours to fly to Washington, D.C. with a short stop in Alaska for refueling. When we landed in Alaska, I was back in America and only about nine hours away from Andrews Air Force Base and Walter Reed Hospital.

It was great to see the snow, so much different than the hot hundred-degree days stomping around the jungles of Vietnam. While we were on land, I was able to get some coffee and breakfast since it was early morning in Alaska.

Robert M. Braun, Sr.

We took off around 0630 to head to Washington, D.C. I settled in for the long ride home glued to the window, happy and relieved that I had survived. I had decided to use my experiences to better myself and relish how lucky I was. I had proven that I was a fighter. Now, I must be determined to fulfill my agreement and promises with Jack, to begin college and eventually have a family.

As the hours flew by, I watched us fly over the Great Lakes and knew I was back in America. As we approached Washington, D.C. I saw the Washington Monument and remembered climbing it when on my senior class trip. I watched as we flew into the airport. I could see the White House, the Capitol buildings, and the Lincoln Memorial. Knowing I would be stationed somewhere around Washington, D.C. for a little more than a year, I promised myself that I would visit all the national monuments. We landed at Andrews Air Force Base almost the same time I left Japan.

Andrews AFB and Joint Base Andrews are named for Lieutenant General Frank Maxwell Andrews (1884–1943), former Commanding General of United States Forces in the World War II European Theater Operations. General Andrews organized and commanded the General Headquarters, Air Force (1935–1939), and at the time of his death on May 3, 1943 in the crash of a B-24 Liberator in Iceland, he was Commanding General, United States Forces, European Theater of Operation. Ref. 43

Waiting for us, were three buses, one for those of us that could walk and two for those on stretchers. Once on the bus I moved to the back and took a seat. Being back in the states was so emotional, that I couldn't help a few tears.

A doctor was in the front seat looking at the medical records of the men on the bus. I was watching the men on stretchers being carried off the back ramp of the C9-A and loaded onto the other buses, feeling for the men who may never walk again, and the ones that would need medical care for the rest of their lives.

The doctor got up and walked back to me and asked if I was, PFC Robert Braun. I answered, "Yes Sir". He said that he was looking at my medical records and was surprised how well I had recovered from my many injuries and told me, I was lucky to be alive. I thanked him and told him it wasn't easy, but I was determined to fight to return to a normal life as quickly as possible.

Andrews Air Force Base was about thirty miles from Walter Reed Army Medical Center and it would take about forty minutes to get there. I was again glued to the window watching the sites as we traveled to the hospital, happy to be back in America.

Walter Reed Army Medical Center from 1909 to 2011 was the medical flagship center for the U. S. Army. It is located in the District of Columbia. The hospital, medical offices, support services, and grounds, cover one hundred and thirteen acres and has served more than one-hundred and fifty thousand retired and active personnel from all branches of the military. The original hospital had a capacity of only eighty patients and grew to about five thousand five hundred rooms and the hospital covered more than twenty-eight acres. Ref. 44

It was named after Major Walter Reed who was an Army physician that led a team that confirmed that mosquitoes transmitted Yellow Fever. Ref. 45

It was just after 0900 hours when the bus arrived at Walter Reed. We all moved off the bus carrying our duffle bags and were directed into a reception room. When an Army nurse, who was registering us into the hospital, saw who I was, told me to call home. She told me that they had been receiving calls from my Father and both Senators from New Jersey, Harrison Williams and Clifford Case, all morning.

After I was registered and assigned a bed, I had to borrow a quarter from one of the nurses and went to a payphone to make a call home. I had gotten the phone number from the nurse and made a collect call.

The phone rang a few times before it was answered. On the other line I heard the voice of my twin brother. I found out later that the whole family was there knowing I would be back that morning and was waiting for my call. They had decided to let my twin brother Rich answer and be the first to talk to me. The memory still brings tears to my eyes more than fifty years later.

After an emotional call home, the family planned to come to Washington, D.C. on the weekend to visit me, and welcome me back. It just so happened that the first family member I saw was my twin brother. He was walking down the hallway with his fiancé Sue. I was returning from getting some x-rays. Somehow, he was able to find me, I guess it was again, twin communication.

We both had tears while we hugged each other, happy we were together again. He told me that if he had been with me, I wouldn't have gotten injured. I couldn't disagree with him but told him that I thought it better I went and not him. The rest of the family were in the waiting room. I got huge hugs from all my family. Many tears of happiness were wept that day.

My fight wasn't over. I still had more than a year of my two years yet to serve, and a little less than a year before the amalgamate plate would be inserted in the hole where the skull had to be removed. Over the next year I was assigned to a few jobs, but severe headaches forced me off the jobs. Then there were the grand mal seizures that began.

The first one I had, when back in the states, was when I had just returned from home on a weekend pass. I was sitting on a bench on the outside of the game room in my barracks, didn't feel well, and went out. I woke up in a bed in Andrew Rader Army Health Clinic, Fort Myer, Arlington, Virginia, and didn't know what had happened.

On December 23rd, 1970, I was re-evaluated at Walter Reed Neurology Clinic, and was diagnosed as having a grand mal type seizure disorder, because an abnormal EEG showed I had atypical brain waves where the shrapnel was located, and the path where it had traveled through the brain. A brain scan also noted an abnormality of the right parieto-occipital area.

The doctor increased the dosage of my Dilantin and added Phenobarbital to control my seizure activity. The medicine helped somewhat, but I still had a few grand mal seizures. They seemed to occur when I was using my eyes a great deal. It was hard to believe that just one year earlier I was guarding the stage for The Bob Hope Christmas Show at Cu Chi in Vietnam.

One happened when on a bus on my way home on a weekend pass. I remembered having a headache and feeling funny. The next thing I remembered was pulling into the bus station in Trenton, New Jersey. There was a big bump on my head and I had bitten my tongue really badly. I called home to have someone pick me up and told them I had a seizure on the way. My Mother picked me up from the bus station. She was extremely concerned about my seizure activity as well as my frequent cephalgia.

Because of my headaches and seizures, I was assigned to clean the men's bathrooms in my barracks. Like I always did, I did the job the best I could. The sergeant in charge thought I did such a good job he would let me leave on a weekend pass after I finished cleaning the bathroom on Thursday morning.

Finally, the three months flashed by and I was scheduled to have the amalgamate plate inserted in the hole where the skull was removed at the end of March, or the beginning of April, 1971. I reported to Walter Reed Hospital as scheduled and the cranioplasty was performed in April 1971.

My parents and Rich came down to the hospital for the operation. A little before I went into the surgical suite, they came into my hospital room. I was able to see them, they wished me luck, and my Mother said she had been praying for me. The operation went well; the prayers must have helped. I now had an amalgamate plate over the hole in my head.

I still had four more months on my two years of military service and ended up not being assigned any duty. I was able to go home on weekend passes, visit the Washington, D.C. museums, and monuments, and was able to be the best man at my twin's wedding.

Finally, about two weeks before my two years of military duty would be over, July 8, 1971, I was sent to the Separation and Transition Program. Near the end of the program the speaker mentioned that if you had a war-related or military injury, you should contact the Veterans Administration when released from the Army to apply for VA disability.

At this point I raised my hand, told the speaker that I had a head injury and other wounds I received while fighting in Vietnam. He was surprised, and told me to speak to him after the lecture. He advised me that I should receive some type of benefits from the Army. I told him that I had been treated at the Andrew Rader US Army Health

Clinic, and he told me I should talk to the doctor who had been treating me. That is exactly what I did.

To make a long story short, after seeing the medical doctor, Joseph B. Fitzgerald, MD, CPT, MC, he submitted forms to the Medical Board of Walter Reed Hospital on July 27th, 1971. On August 9th, 1971 the Physical Evaluation Board concluded that I was physically unfit for duty, and should be released from the Army, permanently retired with a sixty percent disability.

After finding out the decision of the board, I called my Father with the results. I can still remember my Father asking me if I was satisfied with the decision. I told him I was, and just wanted to get out of the Army. On September 1st, 1971, I was released from the Army with an Honorable Discharge, almost two months longer than my two years of service. I was going home, to fulfill my promises to Jack.

The Third Part
is titled: "Make My Point that War and Violence Are Not the Answer".

Robert M. Braun, Sr.

Make My Point that War and Violence Are Not the Answer

The events I witnessed during Vietnam are more proof that war and violence are not the answer. It is why the deaths, and injuries I saw, have inspired me to use the **Power of the Pen** over the years, to write for truths and fight against injustices. The following are five of the many articles in my book, **"Moral Duty"**: all five were published in local newspapers: that use my war experiences to make my point.

Step Across the Line
Printed in Trenton Times, April 2003

Society will take a while to recover from this war of choice. Our Republican leaders have taken our country's overwhelming power which was built with the sweat of its citizens to take our country to war.

I am a survivor of the Vietnam War. Images of children with their legs blown off, enemy soldiers with their bodies torn in half, the feeling of metal passing through my body, and memories of an outer body experience are still fresh in my mind. After going through the horrors of living life at its most primitive state, I can attest to the fact that war is not the answer.

It is not being unpatriotic by disagreeing with our leaders. It is standing up for nonviolence and the only way to stop violence is to use every means to stop it. I believe this administration and the Republicans did not exercise all the options to prevent this war of choice and that is where Bush **"Stepped Across the Line"** between right and wrong.

I agree with Supreme Court Justice Robert L. Jackson, who was this country's representative to the International Conference on Military Trials in August 1945, and the Chief Prosecutor at the Nuremberg War Crimes Trials when he said, *"we must make clear to the Germans that the wrong for which their fallen leaders are on trial is not that they lost the war, but that they started it. And we must not allow ourselves to be drawn into a trial of the causes of the war, for our position is that no grievances or policies will justify resorting to aggressive war. It is utterly renounced and condemned as an instrument of policy."* Ref. 47

Robert M. Braun, Sr.

Bush's actions are more dangerous to society than any depredation that Saddam has means to accomplish. I just hope that the 99% of us that are not in power will take back control of our society, before we move further away from a world where there is no violence and the wealth is shared by all.

Peace Will Not Come with Aggression
Printed in Trenton Times, May 2003

It makes me sad and afraid of the future that so many Americans accepted and believed the administration's reasoning for killing. One of the Ten Commandments is *"Thou shalt not kill"* but, the killing in this war did not seem to matter to so many.

Even people I have been around most of my life have just shrugged their shoulders when it was brought up that thousands have died in this war of choice. What is the difference between killing by suicide attacks or by smart bombs?

Thousands of innocents have died and both sides feel they are justified. I support Representative Charles B. Rangel of Manhattan when he said, *"There is nothing so important to me than the taking of life."*

It is good to see someone taking a stance against killing. I support Senator Kerry of Massachusetts when he said, *"we need a change in leadership: a leadership that will not distort the facts and mislead the American public."* I also support the movement for peace and believe violence will only stop by using every means to stop it: to obtain peace through violence just does not work.

"Peace Will Not Come with Aggression." Shoot first and asking questions later are not acceptable policy internationally, locally, or in the home. We teach our children at the earliest age not to bite or hit. America has become great because it has used a policy of hitting only when attacked.

By striking first, Bush became the aggressor, and with the backing of the people who knows who else we will be fighting. It is dangerous to give anyone so much power.

I can only hope that after the killing is over that America will see that war is not the answer and realize that they have made a mistake in backing this war.

Robert M. Braun, Sr.

Our America has Changed
Published in Trenton Times, December 11, 2005

In reply to the letter "For love of the country", I think that its writer must have spent the last few years in Vice President Dick Cheney's bunker or watching Fox News too much. He must not know that America initiated a war of aggression and has authorized the use of torture.

The post-World War II Nuremberg Tribunal declared: *"To initiate a war of aggression ... is the Supreme International Crime."* UN Secretary General Kofi Annan and the International Commission of Jurists have called the war illegal, as have many Americans.

Torture not only tarnishes the image of America; it also puts our own troops in jeopardy. Information acquired through torture is notoriously unreliable, and above all, torture is morally wrong.

I carry around shrapnel from a hand grenade throughout my body and my head from defending America in Vietnam. At one time, I thought that America was a compassionate and generous country, but under this administration, America has turned into an aggressive, immoral, arrogant country that is destroying everything for which we once proudly stood.

Therefore, I suggest the letter writer stop looking through rose-colored glasses; then he might appreciate the Coalition for Peace Action, which continues to fight for what our country once was: the most benevolent and peace-loving country on the face of the earth.

Administration Puts Nation at Risk
Published in Trenton Times, January 14, 2006

I am responding to the letter, "Not in our nation's best interest" (Dec. 28, 2005). It's writer believes that the Democratic Party leadership wouldn't hesitate to put Americans at risk from terrorists to win an election or to bring down the president.

Almost all of the Democrats that he thinks are putting our country in jeopardy and are against the military, have already protected our nation while serving in the military.

Robert M. Braun, Sr.

The writer thinks that individuals such as Vice President Dick Cheney, House Speaker Dennis Hastert, R-Ill., Tom DeLay, R-Texas, Roy Blunt, R-Mo., Senate Majority Leader Bill Frist, Trent Lott, R-Miss., former U.S. Attorney General John Ashcroft, presidential advisor Karl Rove, Neo-Con Richard Perle, and Paul Wolfowitz, President of the Board of World Bank, who found numerous reasons to get out of serving our country in the military, are now the only ones that can protect it.

It seems that the writer is blindly defending a group of individuals that are using people like him to change our system of government.

There is a name for a system of government that wages aggressive war, tortures prisoners, lies to its citizens, violates their rights, abuses power, breaks the law, rejects judicial and legislative checks, claims unlimited power, and acts in secret. It is called a **Dictatorship**.

As a disabled Veteran, I support the Democrats in their effort against Bush and his administration. I hope that Americans will vote out the Republican's, "Culture of Corruption", and begin impeachment proceedings against Bush and his men.

Lesson of War: It Isn't the Answer

Published in Trenton Times, January 11, 2007

This is in response to the letter, "Fight this War with Total Commitment" (Jan. 7, 2007). One of the writer's recommendations was that we bomb Iraq like we did Japan to end World War II. He goes on to say that America lost more than 60,000 (actual number was 58,220) lives in Vietnam and that combat veterans are lucky if they make it to the age of 60. He continues by complaining that there are too many bleeding-heart liberals in this country and demands that the bashing of President Bush be stopped.

As another disabled combat decorated veteran who was given the last rites twice while in Vietnam, it could only be said that it is sad and unfortunate that the letter writer did not learn, during his tour, that violence and war are not the answer and that peace will not come from violence.

165

The letter writer displays no concern that more than 3,000 Americans have been killed, along with hundreds of thousands of innocent Iraqis. It does not seem to matter to him that hundreds of billions of dollars have been wasted in a war based on lies and that our country is weaker because of the war in Iraq.

After living through the horrors of life at its most primitive, I can attest that war is not the answer. One can only hope that the writer breaks out of his Neo-Con shell and realizes that we bleeding-heart liberals are what got us out of Vietnam and are now trying to get us out of another mistake, Iraq.

Just one more thing: Bush is the worst president this country has ever had.

The Fourth Part

is devoted to keeping my lost friend and fellow
point man's memories alive.

Robert M. Braun, Sr.

Dedicated to Jack Rae Smith

Jack's senior graduation picture.

Jack in Basic Training.

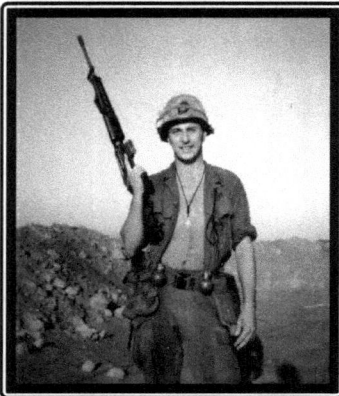

Jack in Vietnam in battle gear.

Jack Rae Smith

SGT-Army Selective Service
25th Infantry Division
20 years old, single, Caucasian, male
Born 04/18/49
From Clarion, Iowa
His Tour of duty Began on 11/26/69
In Dinh Duong, South Vietnam
Ho Stile, Ground Casualty
Multiple Fragmentation Wounds
Body was Recovered
Religion
Church of Christ.

Jack Rae Smith

Visit my friend and others who gave the ultimate sacrifice at the
Vietnam Veterans Memorial in Washington, D.C.
Jack's name is on **Panel 12W, Line 63.**

Visit my friend.

Jack's Home

Those interested in or want to donate to
the
Jack Rae Smith Scholarship at
Wartburg College
should contact:
Wartburg College
Development Office
P.O. Box 1003
Waverly, IA 50677
1-319-352-8495

Jack Rae Smith Scholarship
Scott Leisinger
Vice President for Institutional
Advancement
Phone number: 319-415-1387
Email: scottleisinger@wartburg.edu.

Wartburg College

Is a private Lutheran Liberal Arts College in Waverly, Iowa and has an additional campus, Wartburg West in Denver, Colorado.

The college was founded by Bavaria native Pastor Georg M. Grossmann in 1852 in Saginaw, Michigan. He was sent there to start a training school for German immigrants by Pastor Wilhelm Lohe. The college was moved many times until it was permanently located to Waverly, Iowa in 1935.

The campus is one hundred and eighteen acres. It's colors are orange and black and as of the fall of 2022, has 1,563 students. The Liberal Arts College is for undergraduates aimed at teaching general knowledge and raising intellectual capacities. It has been ranked in the top tier of liberal arts colleges in the country for many years, and offers generous financial aid to almost all students. Ninety-seven percent of their graduates, within six months, have landed a job or go to graduate school, which is among the highest in the state.

If you are interested in finding out more about Wartburg College, their web site is: www.wartburg.edu.

The following is about the **Jack Rae Smith Scholarship.**

On the following page, you will find a letter from Scott Leisinger, Vice President for Institutional Advancement at Wartburg College. See Scott Leisinger's October 10, 2022 letter for qualification requirements.

Robert M. Braun, Sr.

10/10/2022

Dear Robert,

Thank you for your recent telephone call and for your interest in Jack Rae Smith in '71. As per our institutional practice, Jack is considered an alumnus of Wartburg College with his class year (i.e. anticipated graduation year) being 1971, based on his enrollment of at least one academic year. In reality, of course, Jack withdrew after his first year at Wartburg.

The push for an endowed scholarship in Jack's honor came from John Thalacker '65, a fellow Viet Nam veteran and longtime supporter of his alma mater. John had been involved in efforts to pay tribute to another Wartburg alumnus and fallen soldier in Viet Nam, and when he learned of Jack's situation and his connection to Wartburg College, he wanted to do the same for Jack.

In addition to lending financial support, John met with Jack's Clarion (Iowa) High School Class of 1967 classmates, who spread the word to raise gifts to celebrate and sustain Jack's legacy. When the group raised $25,000, an anonymous donor stepped forward to match their generosity, resulting in the creation of the $50,000 Jack Rae Smith Memorial Scholarship. Since the fund is endowed, with investment earnings used to fund the annual scholarship, it will last in perpetuity.

We dedicated a bronze plaque honoring Jack Rae Smith in our Vogel Library at Homecoming, 2017. Thus far, there have been three recipients of the scholarship who have graduated from Wartburg College, including the most recent recipient, Carlos Montez '22.

The scholarship is awarded to: **1.)** A former Wartburg student returning to Wartburg after U.S. Military service in which he/she has been honorably discharged; **2.)** A child of a Wartburg graduate who died in combat; **3.)** A student who is a veteran of the U.S. Armed Forces who has been deployed to any combat or peace-keeping mission for a normal tour; **4.)** A child of a Wartburg graduate who served in combat; or **5.)** A child whose parent served in combat.

Thanks again for your interest, and your service!
Sincerely,
Scott Leisinger
Vice President for Institutional Advancement

Jack's Memories Live on...

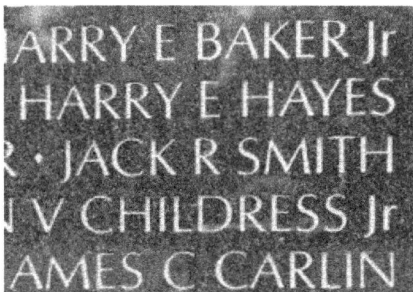

Jack's name on the Vietnam Wall.

My son Rob and grandson Andrew tracing Jack's name from the Vietnam Wall in Washington, D.C.

This is their tracing of Jack's name from the Vietnam Wall.

Scott Case visiting Jack's grave.

Scott Case visiting Jack's grave after their 55th Year Class Reunion. 6/11/2022

Robert M. Braun, Sr.
Friends team up to revive fallen Iowa soldier's memory:
It is a great piece about a great guy.

Friends Team up to Revive Fallen Iowa Soldier's Memory

November 10, 2015

Sgt. Jack Smith from Clarion, Ia., is pictured in March 1970 in Vietnam -- the same month he died in combat just weeks before his 21st birthday.

Those who knew and loved Jack Rae Smith still think of him, a soldier killed in combat 45 years ago in Vietnam just before he turned 21.

"There isn't a day that goes by that he doesn't dance through my mind in some way," said Pam Hagan, 67, who lives in Minneapolis and was Smith's high school sweetheart. They graduated in 1967 from Clarion High School.

But nearly half a century later, Smith's classmates began to worry that the example of his character and accomplishments — whether as a star athlete on the football field or a hero on the battlefield — would be lost.

RELATED: Iowa Vietnam Veteran Casualties

So, something remarkable happened in recent months, almost as if Smith refused to fade into obscurity as a forgotten veteran: A series of conversations and chance encounters — not all of them initially connected, aligned to ensure that Smith's legacy lives on to encourage modern veterans:

1. There's a push to revive the "Jack Smith Award", a humble sports title that had been bestowed on a "most valuable athlete" in each of six sports at Clarion High School (now Clarion-Goldfield-Dows).

Rather than a giant slab of polished black marble, this veteran's memorial had been modest: a wooden plaque whose

174

surface gradually was filled with 60 tiny gold nameplates. The Jack Smith Award was given annually for a decade starting in 1972 but eventually relegated to a dusty corner of the school.

A "most valuable athlete" trophy memorializing high school athlete Jack Smith, killed in Vietnam, was filled with the names of students from 1971 to 1981 at Clarion High School but then forgotten. Jack's classmates, friends and family now are trying to begin a new trophy in his honor.
KYLE MUNSON/THE REGISTER

2. A new memorial scholarship in Smith's honor will be available to active-duty members of the military or honorably discharged veterans who attend Wartburg College in Waverly. Smith studied and played football at Wartburg for a year, then withdrew at the start of his sophomore year in September 1968 to be drafted and deployed to Vietnam.

At first he was wounded in January 1970 and briefly returned home. After redeployment, Smith was killed in combat March 31, 1970.

The sergeant and his platoon had been dropped into Binh Duong Province by helicopters to sweep the area. Suddenly they confronted enemy soldiers fortified in bunkers. Smith was walking "point", or first man in file. According to a fellow soldier, Smith already had walked over a well-concealed bunker when the North Vietnamese opened fire, wounding the Iowan in the leg.

Smith's platoon leader, wounded in the same battle, later wrote to the fallen soldier's parents. He described how Smith's body shielded two of his fellow soldiers from a grenade blast, saving their lives.

A lieutenant colonel in a separate letter added that when the grenade landed a few feet away, the former football quarterback "grabbed the grenade and attempted to throw it back at the enemy when it detonated."

News of Smith's death shattered his family and classmates in Clarion.

He made his final trip home to be buried April 10, 1970.

Smith received a cabinet full of medals, including a pair of Purple Hearts and the prestigious Distinguished Service Cross. (The Distinguished Service Cross is second only to the Medal of Honor, with only 13,400 recipients since it was established in 1917.)

"Most of us, we've gone about and lived our lives and done some good things, and maybe not all perfect," said Scott Case, Smith's friend, and classmate. "All of us just realized that he is the figure that allowed us to do that — he and his veteran's service."

The way that Smith's memory for decades has been threaded through so many different lives helps drive home the impact made by each and every veteran.

"When I put the flag out on Flag Day I think of Smitty. I don't know, I think the older we are the more we think about that and wonder what his life would've been like."

Here are some of those voices still in orbit of this one veteran.

RELATED: IOWA'S FALLEN SOLDIERS SINCE 2003
Tom Blecker

For Tom Blecker, Smith was a best buddy and classmate who helped him save a man's life in Clarion shortly before the soldier returned to Vietnam and was killed.

"Bleck" and "Smitty" would go driving in Blecker's 1959 Chevy as Johnny Rivers "Poor Side of Town" blared on the car stereo.

One night shortly before Smith was due to redeploy, the two sat in the car in an alley in downtown Clarion. They watched a local produce warehouse engulfed in flames. The blaze blew out the windows. Then Smith heard a distant voice cry for help.

A fireman had gotten trapped inside. The two friends climbed atop the warehouse roof to reach him through a window. Blecker helped drag the man out while Smith ran to get more help.

"His hands were burnt right down to the bone," Blecker said of the victim. Just weeks later, Smith's death didn't seem real to Blecker.

After that he would spot Smith's father, Don, at the local bar; the sight of the grieving dad sitting there alone tore him up.

"What am I going to go up and talk to him about?"

Wendell Mayes

For Wendell Mayes, Smith was a savior.

"Jack was a cocky little stinker," said Mayes, 73, who still lives just outside of Clarion. "Good athlete. Quick. Friendly. Got along with most everybody that I know of."

Mayes was the volunteer firefighter who survived a 1970 blaze at a local produce factory thanks to rescue by Smith and Tom Blecker. More than one third of his body suffered severe burns. He spent seven weeks in the hospital in Iowa City and didn't return to work (as an electric lineman) for a year.

Mayes wrote to Smith in Vietnam.

"I told him to keep his ass down and I'd see him when he got home and we'd have a beer," Mayes said. "And it didn't work out."

Smith died before he read the letter, which made its way to the dead soldier's parents in a box of personal items shipped from Vietnam.

"Nothing was solved," Mayes said of the Vietnam War. "Fifty-eight thousand guys' names are on a stone wall in Washington, D.C. That's all that ever came out of it. There was nothing good that came out of that war."

Mayes calls Smith a hero, he said, "not because he saved my rear end. Anyone who went over there I have nothing but respect for them."

Scott Case

For Scott Case, Smith was his teammate in five sports.

Case and Jack befriended each other at age 4. They sacked groceries side by side at the store that Case's parents owned — and where Smith's mom worked as a cashier.

There were two main social groups in Clarion in the 1960s, sort of like "West Side Story": the jocks and "the boys." Smith bridged the two worlds.

Case, 66, today is a real estate agent in the Quad Cities. Half a century ago he bleached his hair blond to sing in a local rock band called the Exiles. Smith would tag along to gigs.

Case tried to sing "How Great Thou Art" at Smith's funeral but broke down in tears. He and Smith had sung that song together atop a mountain in Estes Park, Colo., during a Fellowship of Christian Athletes camp.

"I go out and put flags on Jack's grave each time I go home," Case said.

Pam Hagan

For Pam Hagan, Smith was her high school sweetheart. Hagan, 67, lives in Minneapolis where she helps run Rush City Food Shelf. She was Pam Burt when she and Smith met in seventh grade and soon began dating. They grew apart after high school but continued to correspond even after Smith deployed.

"Jack would always circle back to Pam," said their classmate, Dennis Hoffman.

In his letters from Vietnam, Smith complained to Hagan about shortage of ammunition and other woes.

"I was in such an emotional fog," she said about her reaction to his death, "that I really don't remember that whole week after I was told."

"I didn't know grief could do that to a person."

She's still mad, Hagan said. She moved to Europe for a dozen years after Smith's death as she coped with the entire notion of the war that scarred her generation.

"When I traveled the world I kept looking for him in airports," she said of Smith.

Larry Delano

For Larry Delano, Smith was the Air Force recruit who got away.

Delano, 66, a retired Air Force master sergeant who now lives on Lake Cornelia northeast of Clarion, was stationed at Offutt Air Force Base in Nebraska when high school pal Smith phoned and asked him to visit him at college in Waverly.

Smith was contemplating dropping out of college to be drafted into the Army at the height of the Vietnam War. Unsure of which direction to turn next in life, he sought Delano's counsel.

Four years alive is better than two years dead, Delano pleaded with his friend. He then tried to convince Smith to call his Air Force recruiter in Fort Dodge.

"I thought I had him talked into it," Delano said. But Smith opted for the Army.

"I remember standing on the steps of the church when they brought the casket down," Delano said of the funeral," and I think that was probably the hardest I've ever cried in my life."

Dennis Hoffman

For Dennis Hoffman, Smith and his combat death epitomized the tragic horror of the Vietnam War.

Hoffman, now a professor at the University of Nebraska at Omaha, remembers his classmate as a "gutsy guy" who came from working-class stock and was "one of the archetypes for the jocks" in Clarion.

As a long-haired Vietnam War protester, Hoffman's experience at Smith's funeral seemed surreal.

"Here I am carrying the casket of my teammate in high school," he said. "I had to hold it together just because I wanted to be respectful to Jack. ... But I really just wanted to make some really profane gestures or call out some antiwar slogans."

"It was so farcical that this guy had to die — for what? For nothing."

Kim Arens

For Kim Arens, Smith was "the most awesome uncle you could ever imagine."

Arens, Smith's niece, lived in Marion and stayed with her uncle in Clarion just before he returned to Vietnam for the last time.

"Whenever we would come for a visit," Arens said from California where she now lives, "even though he was very popular he would always take me out on his dates. Always included me. He was a superb human being."

Arens remembers their final conversation. She woke up her uncle in the morning.

"Kim," he told the little girl, "either I'm going to come back with both of my legs or I'm not going to come back at all."

Craig Bergstrom

For Craig Bergstrom, Smith was a towering sports hero. Bergstrom, now chief financial officer for the Kum & Go chain of convenience stores, was just 10 years old when Smith died. His dad, Wayne, was the longtime school football coach. So Bergstrom looked up to Smith and his fellow high school athletes of the late 1960s as sports gods under his dad's guidance.

Smith's funeral was the first funeral he remembers attending.

A couple months ago, Bergstrom, back at his old school in Clarion, glanced at the spot on the wall above the trophy case just outside the gymnasium where the Jack Smith Award had been prominently displayed. It was gone. Only then did Bergstrom discover that Smith's award had been dormant for decades.

It was fate or luck that inspired Bergstrom to duck his head into a storage room as he wandered the hallways. He spotted a box in the corner. He bent down and pulled out the Smith trophy.

The school board let Bergstrom take home the award. It now hangs on his office wall at home in Johnston as he has joined the effort to launch a new Jack Smith Award.

John Thalacker

For John Thalacker, Smith was a veteran whose memory should endure even among those whom he never met.

Thalacker, 73, is a Wartburg College alumnus and Vietnam veteran who spent 24 years as an Iowa prison warden.

He never met Smith; he only heard about him by chance a couple years ago in a conversation. Thalacker had believed that only one Wartburg student had been killed in Vietnam; now here was Smith, a second casualty with ties to the college. He conducted his own research and came away impressed at the young man's record.

"I don't want his memory to be lost in the jungle of Vietnam," he resolved.

Thalacker began work to establish a scholarship in Smith's honor. He joined forces with the soldier's family and Clarion classmates.

"I'm a proud Vietnam veteran," Thalacker said of his stance on the controversial war. "I make no qualms about that. I did what I was asked to do. Even when I went, I thought, 'If I survive this, I am going to be a better man for it.'"

180

Robert M. Braun, Sr.

Thalacker summed up the lesson he sees in Smith's legacy: "One person can go decide to do something and make big things happen."

POSTED ON 10.15.2013
POSTED BY: **CRAIG BERGSTROM**

MY HERO
You were the star QB and my dad was your coach. I played baseball with you and Scott Case on 4th street in Clarion when I was about 8 years old. You and I are the only ones in school history to letter in 5 different sports. Your funeral was so sad and my first. I think of you often and visit your grave in Clarion every time I go back. You were special and a hero to this once 8-year-old boy from small town Clarion, IA.

POSTED ON 3.31.2021

POSTED BY: A GRATEFUL VIETNAM VET

DISTINGUISHED SERVICE CROSS AWARD

CITATION:
The President of the United States of America, authorized by Act of Congress, July 9, 1918 (amended by act of July 25, 1963), takes pride in presenting the Distinguished Service Cross (Posthumously) to Specialist Fourth Class Jack Rae Smith, United States Army, for extraordinary heroism in connection with military operations involving conflict with an armed hostile force in the Republic of Vietnam, while serving with Company B, 2nd Battalion, 12th Infantry, 25th Division, United States Army. Specialist Four Smith distinguished himself by exceptionally valorous actions on 31 March 1970 while on a sweep mission in Binh Duong Province. Specialist Smith was providing forward security for his patrol when an intense barrage of hostile fire was directed at the group from a nearby enemy element. From his forward position, Specialist Smith placed suppressive fire on the enemy that enabled his

comrades to move forward. As his comrades neared his position, an enemy grenade landed a few feet from Specialist Smith. Without hesitation, he seized the grenade and attempted to hurl it back toward the enemy soldiers. However, before he could release the grenade, it detonated in his hand, mortally wounding him. Although Specialist Smith forfeited his own life, he successfully shielded his nearby comrades from the deadly shrapnel and prevented any additional loss of life. Specialist Four Smith's extraordinary heroism and devotion to duty, at the cost of his life, were in keeping with the highest traditions of the military service and reflect great credit upon himself, his unit, and the United States Army.

Jack's Gravestone

Jack is buried at Evergreen Cemetery,
Highway 3, Clarion, Iowa 50525
Visit My Friend

The Fifth Part

has pictures taken by me, as well as photographs of FSB Pershing, FSB Kien, and The Bob Hope Christmas Show.

Pictures taken by me.

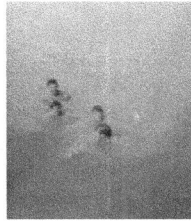

These four photos are from an assignment where my platoon spent the day traveling up the Saigon River to destroy a VC camp. It is where I fired an anti-tank rocket launcher at one of the VC bunkers to destroy it. This was also one of the best days I spent in Vietnam. After destroying the VC camp, we were able to dive off the boats and swim in the Saigon River.

Jack and a few guys relaxing and having a few beers.

This is Tennessee, the 60-cal machine gunner for the 2nd squad.

Brownie and Jack

Members of my unit with some village children.

These are some of the members of my platoon.

This is a picture of mortar rounds being fired outside FSB Pershing at suspected VC.

Robert M. Braun, Sr.

Pictures of Cu Chi.

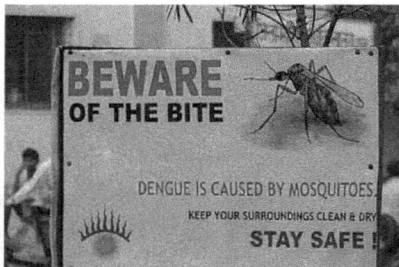

Cu Chi Base Camp Entrance

Kính chào quý khách !
WELCOME TO THE CU CHI TUNNELS!

BEWARE OF THE BITE
DENGUE IS CAUSED BY MOSQUITOES.
KEEP YOUR SURROUNDINGS CLEAN & DRY
STAY SAFE !

Pictures of FSB Pershing.

This is the mess hall where we ate breakfast and dinner when in FSB Pershing.

Award Ceremony like the one Jack and I had when receiving our first Purple Hearts.

Pictures of FSB Kien

This is a mortar that was used both day and night to protect the men in the field.

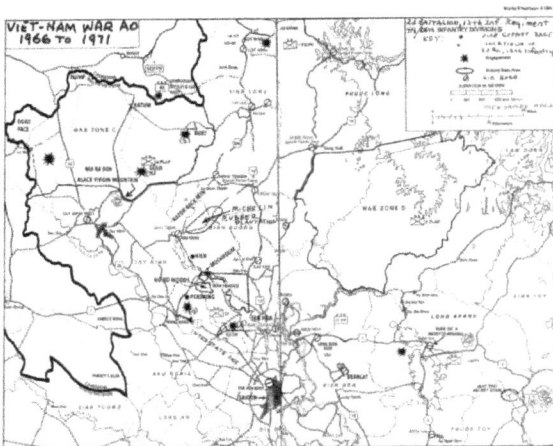

This is a map of the area we patrolled showing FSB Pershing, FSB Kien and FSB Pine Hill, also known as the Black Virgin Mountain.

Bunker on the line Bravo Co. This is the location of my hooch.

Robert M. Braun, Sr.
Pictures of The Bob Hope Christmas Show

190

The Sixth Part

includes examples of my other writings from four Children's books, "Moral Duty", and "Hitting Drills and Much More".

Published Books by Robert M. Braun, Sr.

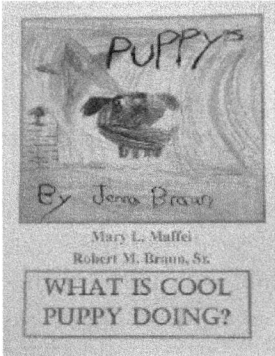

Retail book Price $13.99
Book is 8.5 x 11 inches.
ISBN: 978-1-890007-08-9

What is Cool Puppy Doing? is co-authored by my seven-year-old granddaughter Jenna M. Braun and Mary L. Maffei. Jenna is the artist and creator of the picture on the cover.

What is Cool Puppy Doing? is designed for children: to help them learn to read, know shapes, numbers, colors, important signs, and their favorite vegetables and fruits, displays twenty various occupations, and gives the child the opportunity to choose what they want to do when they grow up: as well as giving the child a place to color and name the pictures they color. This book is appropriate for children in pre-school through fourth grade.

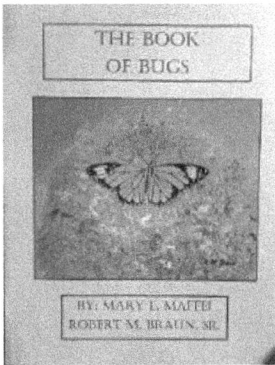

Retail book Price $13.99
Book is 8.5 x 11 inches.
ISBN: 978-1-890007-13-3

The Book of Bugs is co-authored by Mary L. Maffei.

The Book of Bugs is an educational tool to help the young reader, learn to read, the alphabet, count to fifty, sound out words, recognize street signs, name the planets, and build word vocabulary. The book is a delightful, beautifully illustrated interactive book that builds children's confidence in basic literacy and decision-making skills. It generates creative thinking while strengthening bonds with the parent, teacher, grandparent, and anyone reading with the child. This book is appropriate for children in pre-school through fourth grade. The picture on the cover is an acrylic painting by Robert M. Braun, Sr.

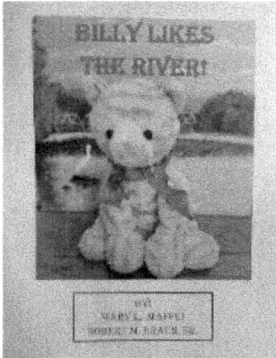

Retail book Price $13.99
Book is 8.5 x 11 inches.
ISBN: 978-1-890007-12-6

Billy Likes the River is co-authored by Mary L. Maffei.

Billy Likes the River is an interactive book that is designed to advance and create the foundation for healthy learning and the development of the child. It helps the child learn the skills they need for life, like: communicating, thinking, problem-solving, and being with others.

The book starts with learning the alphabet, both upper and lower case, and counting to fifty. It helps the child to read aloud and sound out words, which are both educational social tools and skills needed by the young reader. The book introduces them to simple addition and encourages the young reader to use their fingers, if necessary, to help solve addition problems, all while being coached by their friend, Billy. The book *Billy Likes the River* provides encouragement to young readers to use their creativity skills to name the pictures they color. This book is appropriate for children in pre-school through fourth grade.

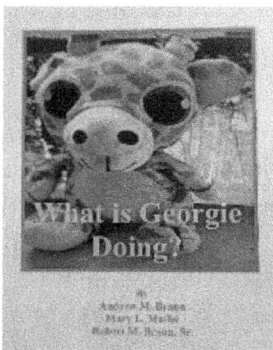

Retail book Price $13.99
Book is 8.5 x 11 inches.
ISBN: 978-1-890007-11-9

What is Georgie Doing? is co-authored by my nine-year old grandson Andrew M. Braun and Mary L. Maffei.

What is Georgie Doing? is an interactive book that is designed to advance and create the foundation for healthy learning and the development of the child. It helps the more advanced child learn the skills they need for life, like: communicating, thinking, problem-solving, and being with others. It provides two places for the child to learn multiplication. The book provides encouragement to young readers to use their creativity skills to name the pictures they color. It contains a page where

194

Georgie is against all kinds of Racism and Discrimination, a place for the child to pick their favorite sign and five pages for the child to color pictures pertaining to racism, of all kinds. This book is appropriate for children in pre-school through fourth grade.

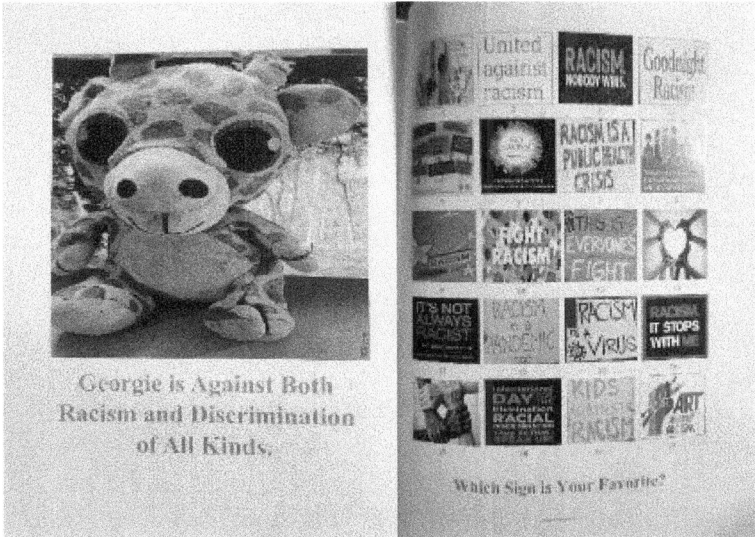

Georgie is Against Both Racism and Discrimination of All Kinds.

Which Sign is Your Favorite?

All four childrens' books are a welcome addition to any child's library for both your young children or grandchildren.

You can order them from Amazon, other book stories and from **River Magic Publishing**. See directions below.

Robert M. Braun, Sr.

Hitting Drills and Much More

Hitting Drills and Much More was originally self-published in 1996 and the second edition was published in February 2021, by IUniverse. The picture on the cover is a colored pencil drawing by my twin brother, Richard J. Braun.

Paperback Price $17.99   eBook $3.99
  Book is 8.5 x 11 inches. Both paperback and eBook
  ISBN- 978-1-6632-1859-9   available on Amazon

This is what was said about **"Hitting Drills and Much More"**:

An article in the September 1997 Babe Ruth Bullpen… "as the title implies, is much more than just a manual designed to help correct many common hitting mistakes like: stepping in the bucket, over-striding, and lunging. It also provides valuable information regarding the development and management of ballplayers. **"Hitting Drills and Much More"** is a book about keys to success."

Hopewell Valley News:... "a book that makes people feel good about life—themselves. Enjoy the sunrises and sunsets, take time to sit back and relax, appreciate quality family time, slow down, and admire the beauty around us. That's where the Much More, comes from."

"Hitting Drills and Much More" is designed to help educate those who know little about baseball/softball as well as help develop better ballplayers and managers. It is simple enough for a new player, and sophisticated enough for the most advanced. It is a usable tool for the first-year coach to the seasoned veteran, so all can benefit by reading and using many of the ideas and drills shown in the manual.

Here are samples from the book.

Introduction

This hitting drill manual/book is designed to help correct many common hitting mistakes such as stepping in the bucket and casting. It also provides valuable information regarding the development and management of ballplayers: such as the simple task of choosing the right bat to the ultimate ingredients for hitting success, and forty-five hitting drills. It is simple enough for a new player and sophisticated enough for the most advanced player. It is a usable tool for the first-year coach to the seasoned veteran. All can benefit by reading and using many of the ideas and drills shown in the manual.

It's so easy for hitters to fall into bad habits and these bad habits can be corrected only by repeating the correct hitting mechanics demonstrated. When performing these drills, it is extremely important that each drill be performed correctly because research has shown that it takes seventeen correct muscle movements to correct one wrong movement. Therefore, the earlier the correct muscle movement can be programmed into the brain, the easier it will be to become a good hitter.

This manual will fill a void in the basic baseball skill development market. In bookstores and libraries, most baseball books are about present or past professional baseball players. Most are great stories but few provide the necessary instructions for the development of ballplayers and managers.

The Art of Coaching – is a collection of short articles published in a newsletter, by Robert M. Braun. Each is designed to help get the most out of each player.

Bat Selection — explains how to choose the correct bat. It explains why there are different types of bats, gives a method on how to determine the correct weight bat, and how to deal with wooden bats when reaching pro ball.

Grip – gives examples of the best method to hold a bat and how much grip pressure should be applied when hitting.

Plate coverage — explains why it is so important to get into the same spot in the batter box every time and explains how to use the bat as a measuring tool.

Strike Zone Discipline – explains why the hitter should swing at strikes.

Ultimate Ingredients for Hitting Success – deals with the recipe of ingredients from desire to visual reminders that are necessary to help develop a good mental approach towards becoming a good hitter.

Basic Offensive Strategy – emphasizes the need and reasons for a total team effort and responsibilities needed by each player to score runs and win ball games.

Basic Hitting Philosophy – deals with the interaction of swing mechanics, concentration, confidence, and strike zone discipline, how they work together and basic goals every hitter should have.

Hitting Philosophies & Theories – deals with working on muscle memory and working to be a good hitter.

Mental Skills for Hitters – explains the importance of the mental side of hitting, taking mental inventory, active awareness, and reframing.

Running a Good Practice – gives examples of good practice routines, infield and bunting drills, and advanced hitting routine.

Situation Hitting – gives the Offensive strategies for different situations like: what to do with runner held at first, lead-off hitter in the game, runner on third with less than two outs, and more. This chapter is designed to coordinate the offensive strategy of both manager and player.

Hitting Drills – details   forty-five different hitting drills designed to help correct hitting mistakes like stepping into the bucket, casting, and many more.

Becoming a Pro – includes Steve Braun Pinch-hitter deluxe, Doctor Stroke, The Trump Card, and what made Steve a fifteen-year professional major league baseball player.

Baseball Statistics – provides basic statistics used to evaluate players and teams.

The Brothers' Story – is a little bit about Steve, Rich, and Bob.

Art of Coaching 1

Many years ago, when learning the game of baseball, I can remember my Father telling my brothers and me, that the most important job of a coach is getting the most out of each player. With that philosophy, the success of a coach's ability is not measured by win/loss record; it is measured by how much improvement each player makes during the season.

This philosophy translates into more than hoping a young player improves. It means spending time with your players at practice and emphasizing that the game is played not just to win but also for fun. It means continually gaining knowledge and improving as a coach. Practice should include drills that keep every player moving and involved. Words of encouragement and praise should be given even if mistakes are made. Always look for the positive and build from there.

If young players feel good about themselves, they are willing to learn. Their play will improve as confidence increases. It's important that confidence be built at an early age, so a coach should always balance playing time and position with ability. Let the young player improve and grow before placing them in critical positions like pitcher, catcher, shortstop, or first base. Remember, you are building a person, so be patient, work hard, and always give words of encouragement. Make the game fun for both you and your players.

> The book has forty-five hitting drills to help solve many hitting problems. Here are two examples.

DRILLS

Problem: Poor Balance in Stance

Drill 1: Jump up and land

Player gets into their stance and jumps vertically while maintaining his/her stance. When he/she reaches the ground, they should feel connected to the ground with a solid leg base.

Drill 2: Pushover

Attempt to pushover the player from all angles, front, back, and both sides. Try to surprise him/her with your push. This will check his/her stability. If he/she has stability and balance, emphasize that they are connected to the ground with their feet.

The Brothers' Story

The three brothers, Steve, Rich, and Bob grew up in the small town of Titusville, New Jersey and lived in a place called Washington Crossing, New Jersey. They are the oldest of nine children: four boys and five girls. Steve is the oldest born nine months one day before identical twins Rich and Bob. Rich was born ten minutes before Bob and was the heaviest weighing three pounds fifteen ounces and Bob three pounds thirteen ounces.

They spent many hours growing up playing basketball and baseball in their backyard and neighborhood. All three played Little League, Babe Ruth baseball, and varsity basketball for their high school. Steve went on to play High School varsity baseball and was drafted after high school. He went on to play fifteen years in the Major Leagues, then was a coach in the Minor Leagues for a number of years as indicated in the story about him, "**Becoming a Pro**".

Rich and Bob went on to play years of slow pitch softball. All three were successful because they wanted to be good by practicing the game they loved to play. Always first to practice, last to leave, and playing the game, as if they had a one run lead no matter the score, helped all three have successful sports careers.

Rich was also a great artist that was featured on covers of national magazines, see the following part about Rich. Rich was a pitcher that at one time was one of the best around. If you place the box the softball came in on the plate, Rich could throw a high ark pitch right into the box.

Their practice field, when growing up, was/is an old schoolyard at the old Titusville Grammar School overlooking the Delaware River. Here is a story by Bob about the old practice field where they practiced with their Father. Bob also used the field to practice with his daughters Kim, Emily, and son Rob. Now, the old schoolyard is being used to practice with Bob's grandchildren, Andrew, and Jenna.

The Old Schoolyard

Take me out to the old ballfield, echoes on the red bricks of the old school. Hopefully another pro will outgrow the fences that were out of reach not long ago.

Many feet have run across the aged green grass that still makes a good field. There goes another pitch of many buckets of balls that have seen the face of the bat, too many to count.

Years ago, working with my brothers, waiting for my turn to hit, I can still remember enjoying the practices, and having fun. How I've enjoyed watching us all grow living different lives. How proud I am to have them play with my kids, Kim, Rob, and Emily, as well as my grandchildren Andrew, and Jenna.

The field would be proud of the successes lived by many laughing children that fell, cried, and loved being free to run on it; still here to help me develop the next pro that may come out of the old ballfield.

Some of the things that helped the three become the athletes they became was, their work ethics and the competition between them. To help build strength, their father bought a five-spring exercise apparatus that they used every night to build muscles, starting with one spring and moved on to using all five springs.

They also did jumps every night to increase their jumping ability: first the doorway then eventually the ceiling. Their mother always complained about handprints on the ceiling.

Robert M. Braun, Sr.

Carl, the brothers' younger brother known as the "Shark", won the New Jersey Baseball State Championship his senior year in high school as the shortstop and leadoff hitter. Competition and playing with his older brothers helped him develop his skills. He was called the Shark because of the way he gobbled up ground balls at shortstop.

Bob's son Rob, was also a great ballplayer. He won the batting title his high school senior year with an average of four fifty-five and made The All-Area Baseball Team in the year 2000. This was impressive since his league ended up winning two New Jersey Baseball State Championships.

Baseball is, and has been, a big part of the Braun family.

"HITTING DRILLS AND MUCH MORE"
is available at Amazon, Barnes and Noble, other
book stores, and at:
River Magic Publishing
P.O. Box 8
Titusville, N.J. 08560

Robert M. Braun, Sr.

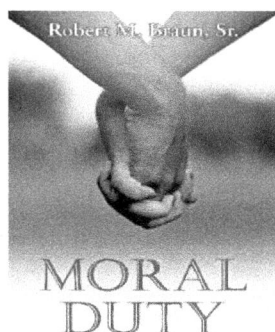

Moral Duty

ISBN: 978-1-890007-16-4 (e)
eBook: $9.00
ISCN 987-1-89000-19-5 (sc)
Softcover: $19.00
ISBN: 978-1-890007-27-0 (hcbw)
Hardcover: $29.99
ISBN: 987-1-890007-28-7 (hcc)
Hardcover: $49.99

MORAL DUTY

The book is a collection of writings over the years of performing my moral duty to fight for truths and against injustice to help advance our world to a better future, while providing a wealth of information in captivating stories: topics range from raising three children as a single parent to losing my identical twin brother to dementia. The book includes stories entitled "Equal Employment for the Disabled", "Look Who's Wearing the Apron", "The Importance of Amino Acids", "Dementia/Alzheimer", "Flat Tax Not Fair", "King's Puppets", "The Nurse the Giver", stories about cancer, autism, givers, greed, Machiavellianism, and has thirty-seven letters that were published in local newspapers. All of these writings are in chapters titled **"Moral Duty/Moral Responsibility"**, **"Power of the Pen"**, **"Diet and Health"**, and **"The Love of Life"**.

These are examples of writings from the book *"Moral Duty"*.

Introduction

Those of us that are living today know more than all that lived before us. We know our earth is special, a **Blue Marble** in the vastness of space. We know more about our bodies, our mind, and how it works, our neighboring planets, and our Universe. We know more about medicine, communication, availability of information, music, nature, space, our world, and so much more. Every day more knowledge becomes available that is at our fingertips. These advancements happen through the work and thinking of gifted humans.

We have learned what has caused the mass extinction of the dinosaurs and that it can happen again. We have learned that our world is at risk from numerous ways of being destroyed. **We, as the only intelligent species**, **isn't it our moral duty** to provide more resources to prevent these disasters from ending our world again, and to provide resources to give every human a chance to reach their full potential? Who knows from where the next great minds will come?

Just imagine, how quickly we have advanced. We as humans have only lived the last three seconds of an hour if the earth's life is measured as an hour. That's right, the last three seconds; how much more we could develop in the next three seconds if the wealth was more evenly divided?

But, there are calls that there is a limited amount of wealth that is available. Yet, fifteen American billionaires have a total of nine hundred and twenty billion five hundred million dollars and the combined net worth of the 2017 class of the 400 richest Americans was $2.7 trillion, up from $2.4 trillion in the previous year. As of 2023 the U.S. had 724 billionaires that have a combined wealth of $4.48 trillion. More wealth is held in a small number of individuals than the masses. Eight individuals, six Americans, have more wealth than half of the human race. Today, a number of individuals are worth 100 billion dollars or more. Why, is it right that so few individuals have SO much while calls are being made, we don't have enough to save our world? (See more on this in chapters on "Moral Duty/Moral Responsibility" and "Power of The Pen")

I have spent the last fifty plus years wondering why I survived the jungles of Vietnam while my friend and fellow point man, Jack Rae Smith did not. (See story "With Me Still"). Over these years I have accepted the responsibilities of raising my three children as a single parent, (See story "Look Who's Wearing the Apron") had writings published that expressed actions I felt were wrong, fought for fairness for the disabled, (See story "Equal Employment for the Disabled") and tried to help others. Many of my writings deal with taxation, disparity of wealth, our wars, and health. It all has come down to my moral duty to help advance our world to a better future. Maybe 100, 1,000, 10,000 years from now my moral duty or yours, will help us get to that better future.

Knowing that I am not the smartest, best athlete, writer, or artist, but I do have something going for me and that is my **life experiences**. These experiences have given me the opportunity to appreciate life and the beauty around us. It has provided my knowledge of our tax policies and how they have been used to shift our wealth to the Kings of Our Time. Also, that there is only so much wealth and when more of it is shifted to a few, the rest of us have less. It's just like pie, when a small group gets more of the pie, there is less for everyone else.

After having an outer body experience and drifting to the light, my moral duty is to speak out for fairness for all and to express this the best way I can; for example, the art of both my twin brother and I, that shows the beauty of life (See chapter "The Love of Life") as well as my writings. My twin brother left this world on November 26, 2013. (See story "Dementia" in the chapter "Diet and Health.")

Over the years I have learned one thing that will help me reach my goals, and that is, to use my experiences to be able to control the ship called Bob. Many times, in the past, I have found myself out of control; to control my seizure disability caused by a head injury received in Vietnam, I began to use biofeedback to understand what was happening within my body. (See story "Biofeedback" in the chapter "Diet and Health")

The characters in the story "Biofeedback", are the crew members of my ship, which helped me overcome the many ups and downs of my life. The great thing about having a crew for my ship is, I can call anyone onto my ship to help me perform my moral duty. This is what I did when I called Aristotle, Benjamin Franklin, Thomas Paine, and George Washington onto my ship by using what they wrote.

Aristotle understood this more than 2000 years ago when he wrote: *"A democracy cannot function if there are extremes of wealth."* Ref. 48

Benjamin Franklin found this out in 1758 when representing the Pennsylvania Assembly to the kings of his time that: *"Those that have the money make the rules."*

This is what both Thomas Paine and George Washington wrote in 1776 when the difficulties for Independence became apparent.

Robert M. Braun, Sr.

Thomas Paine wrote: *"That the harder the conflict, the more glorious the triumph."* Ref. 49

George Washington wrote: *"The cause we are engaged in is so just and righteous, that we must try to rise superior to every obstacle in its support."* Ref. 50 Also, *"It is better to stand alone than in Bad Company".* Ref. 51

It is my, and everyone's moral duty to continue to try to help us reach our future. These writings are something that will transcend time. That is how we know of Socrates, Aristotle, Benjamin Franklin, and many others that have left their mark on history by their writings. Enjoy your reading, and continue to learn and control what is going on inside of your ship. If we all can control our ships and share the wealth of our world, how much further we could travel into our future and into the heavens above.

Speaking Out For Fairness For All

The following five writings: entitled "Freedom" (January 2002), and "Liberals: Our Country was Founded on Liberal Principles" (January 2004), was published in the Trenton Times. The three others: one titled "My Vote", written two weeks before the 2016 election, one entitled "Your Vote", written two weeks after the election of Trump, and "America the Beautiful", written following the 2024 election. These five writings are included in the chapter "Power of the Pen", and as samples here because they reflect some of the reasons I wrote "Moral Duty".

By surviving the jungles of Vietnam, I was inspired to use the power of the pen over the years, to fight against untruths, injustice, discrimination, and inequalities, while standing up for our Constitution and Democracy.

Freedom
Printed in Trenton Times, October 2002

I am writing in regards to the article, "Protesters Register Their Point of View From Afar" in the September 24, 2002 Trenton Times. What struck me the most about the article is not the protesters but what was said about them by the Bush supporters. In particular what was said by Art Ward of Bensalem, PA, when he said, "They should shoot them." Where is the freedom guaranteed in our Constitution when one cannot have conflicting beliefs? Mr. Ward should be arrested and put on trial for terroristic and threatening remarks.

There is no place in a free democracy for one side of an issue to resort to violence if another disagrees with them. All violence must stop because violence only leads to more violence. This will happen more and more as one party continues to increase its power and resort to arrogance by refusing to respect other opinions.

Liberals: Our Country was Founded on Liberal Principles
Printed in Trenton Times, January 2004

This is in response to T. Burnett Fisher's letter to the editor, "Liberals are ruining our country" in December 13, 2003, Trenton Times. The very idea that liberals are ruining this country is naive and without basis. Quite to the contrary, liberal values are based on political equality and economic opportunity. They believe that Democracy is the one form of government that is from the consent of the people, and that the freedoms written in the Bill of Rights, are essential. This commitment to the Bill of Rights is why liberals stand up for women, minorities, gays, immigrants, and other less fortunate groups.

Liberals believe in Democratic Capitalism with a strong central government to protect the interests of society, and that uncontrolled accumulation of wealth and power leads to pollution, fraud, and exploitation of labor. Just check the headlines of newspapers across the country over the past couple of years as evidence of this.

Mr. Fisher, and other like-minded, should remember that liberal policies have made America the most free, wealthiest, most successful, and powerful nation in history: because of policies like the Progressive Era, The New Deal, The Fair Deal, GI Bill, The Great Society, and a private enterprise system that relies on Government safeguards against depression, poverty, and provides society with the opportunities to advance and grow.

Mr. Fisher, if your workplace is safe and your children go to school instead of working, you are paid a living wage, overtime and work a 40-hour week; that your food is safe and water is drinkable; you and your parents are able to receive Medicare and Social Security; your rivers and air are clean; and that different races can gather in public, marry, and vote, you can thank liberals. Conservatism has fought all of these and many other progressive policies, and is now out to destroy society's safety nets: safety nets that ensure that those less fortunate will have an opportunity to take advantage of higher education, medical services, and guard against job loss, and starvation.

Finally, Mr. Fisher, liberal Bush bashing is not being done because he is putting the liberals in jeopardy, but because he represents the Neo-Cons in their attempt to consolidate wealth, to choose war as the first choice, and to weaken government so that it cannot provide political, legal, and social equality that is the practice and spirit of Democracy.

Your right-wing demagoguery is another attempt to label liberals as anything but what they are, defenders of freedom, the less fortunate, and the American way. I am proud to say I am a liberal, disabled Vietnam Veteran, single parent, a twenty-eight-year public employee, that will continue to stand up for non-violence, strong government that protects society, and believe that the wealth of our world should be shared by all.

My Vote
Written two weeks before 2016 election:

I will not vote for a candidate that the white supremacist groups support. During my tour in Vietnam, I served with African Americans and individuals from Central and South America. We were all drafted to serve to fight for our country.

I was injured and nearly killed, and my friend Jack Rae Smith lost his life, and saved mine. (see "With Me Still"). An immigrant carried me to safety, and I shared many scary nights with my black brothers. Racism cannot be allowed in our democracy.

What has made our country great is the melting pot of treating all equal. To believe one race is superior is wrong. We are all humans given the riches of our world to use our intelligence in order to enjoy the beauty of life and to expand beyond our world.

Robert M. Braun, Sr.

We cannot do this when individuals carry hatred to others because they are different colors, believe in other gods, or speak a different language. I will continue to use my vote to elect someone who believes we are better together.

Your Vote
Written two weeks after 2016 election:

To all those who voted for Donald Trump, hate crimes are up because of your choice to elect an immoral racist person. Our democracy has no room for hatred and bigotry. Jews, Muslims, non-whites, and gays are now being targeted by individuals who must belittle others to make themselves feel more important. They lack the mental capacity to understand that we are all equal and require the same things to live.

More Confederate flags are being flown, and that flag represents hatred, racism, and a time when we had to fight to save our nation and free fellow humans from slavery.

We have witnessed what hatred can lead to, where millions were put to death because of their religious beliefs and others were considered property because of their color.

It's really sad that we're heading, because of your vote, to a place where this kind of behavior is acceptable. Your vote has given a voice to white supremacists and other racist groups who deserve no place in our democracy, or our world.

We as a human race will not continue to develop if all are not given the opportunity. We must all come together as a country no matter our color, religion, sexual orientation, or country of our origin to build a better America and world.

I have almost given up on the human race to realize that the only way we are going to continue enjoying the beauty of life is to share the wealth of our world and the heavens above. I fully realize that I am in the autumn of my time and will not witness human maturity. All I can do is help those close to me to realize their potential and to prepare for the future.

The Republicans would get in bed with the devil to get their tax breaks for the wealthy and make sure the government is dysfunctional. They are the same type of person who would and

209

did follow Hitler - blindly, not ever asking what is best for our country and all the people, putting party ahead of country.

America the Beautiful
Written following the 2024 election.

We now have a president that thinks America is the garbage can of the world; a president that has threatened anyone who disagrees with him. A president that has been convicted with thirty-four felonies, has been charged with molesting women, and tried to stop the transfer of our government by inciting an insurrection. Those that have voted for him are responsible for electing him, can now watch a president who does not love America, use his unlimited power to destroy what our forefathers fought for, to make America the Beautiful.

I almost lost my life in Vietnam, was given the last rites twice, and many individuals have lost their lives fighting for our beautiful country of America. I have lived in Washington Crossing, New Jersey, for most of my life and know the sacrifices of those brave men, who crossed the Delaware River on that cold Christmas night on December 25th, 1776, on our way to freedom. I love my country of America and I was proud to call myself an American but, I am now questioning this, because of how morally wrong so many in America are, by electing someone who does not love this great nation.

Now we have a president that believes America is the garbage can of the World. To all that used their vote to elect this immoral president, who does not love our country, I can only hope you are not sorry for your vote, and we still have our Democracy. I suggest you listen to the song: "America the Beautiful" by Ray Charles.

Available as an eBook and soon to be available as a paperback on Amazon

Robert M. Braun, Sr.

Purple Heart Ceremony

Warriors for our Country

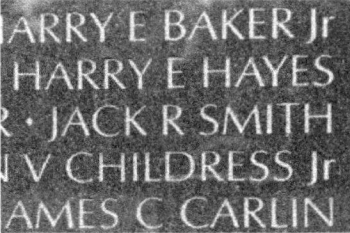
Fallen Soldiers

Washington Crossing

If you are interested in purchasing "Hitting Drills and Much More", and any or all the children's books, send a check or money order, **made out to Bob Braun,** for the total price of the book(s) plus seven dollars (for the entire pkg.) for shipping and handling, along with your address and telephone number.

To: **River Magic Publishing
P O Box 8
Titusville, New Jersey 08560**

"Two Times Dead in Vietnam", and the Childrens' books are available at Amazon, Barnes and Noble, and other book stores.

Upcoming book
Poems Short Stories Art

Retail book Price: $16.99

ISBN: 978-1-890007-1-57 (sc)
ISBN: 978-1-890007-20-x (e)

The book is a collection of poems, short stories, and art that Robert M. Braun, Sr. has created over the years that expresses his love of life: something he learned while surviving the jungles of Vietnam. His near-death experience inspired him to use the power of the pen to write interesting, informative stories, and articles to help others and tell the truth so that hopefully, we could have a better world. He utilizes the brush to show the beauty of life. His poems are designed to be short, easily understood, and are intended to send a message. Here are three examples.

Blue Marble
We have not been thrown out of the garden but into it to enjoy the beauty of life. Where else would you find a blue marble in the vastness of space growing food right out of the ground.

More in Life
I saw and came close to death;
it is why I do more in life.

Say:
A picture is worth a thousand words.
A pen is worth a million guns.

Some of the titles of his short stories are: "With Me Still", "Look Who's Wearing the Apron", "Kim and the Frog", "The Jersey Devil", "Christmas Morning", "The Nurse the Giver", "Autism", "The Three Virtues of Life", "Dementia", "Becoming a Pro". The Bike Trail. The cover is a sample of his art.

Robert M. Braun, Sr.

The Seventh Part
is "About the Author", Washington
Crossing, New Jersey, my home, and
samples of my art.

About the Author:

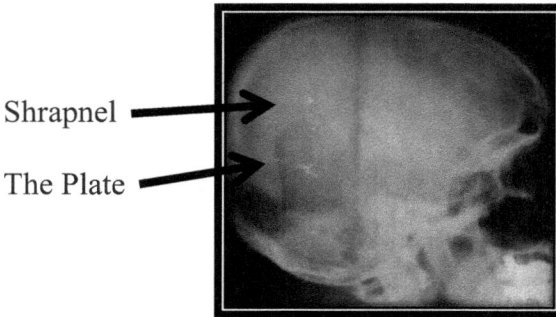

This is an x-ray that shows a plate and shrapnel of one of Bob's injuries while serving in Vietnam.

Robert M. Braun, Sr.

Robert M. Braun, Sr. is a disabled Vietnam veteran who received two Purple Hearts and a Bronze Star Medal for bravery, and was awarded the New Jersey Distinguished Service Medal in 2000. His injuries included a bullet wound to his right bicep, as well as shrapnel wounds to his right leg, groin, back, and head. After he was released from the Army, Bob graduated from Rider University, New Jersey, with a Bachelor of Science in Commerce and a minor in accounting in February of 1977. He then worked for thirty-four years as an auditor for the New Jersey State Treasury Department specializing in inheritance and estate tax and has been retired since May 1, 2010. Working for the state of New Jersey, he gained his vast knowledge of the tax systems.

During this time, he self-published the first edition of *Hitting Drills and Much More* in 1996 and the book titled *A Story of Life* in 2000. He has had thirty-seven letters published in local newspapers to fight against untruths, injustice, discrimination, inequalities. He also had three stories about Vietnam published in a national magazine in the late 1990s. They are "The Sun at Last", "Top of the World, Ma!", and

"With Me Still", and each are a chapter in this book *Two Times Dead in Vietnam*. The story "With Me Still" describes the author's last mission in Vietnam, how he was injured, and how he lost his friend and fellow point man, Jack Rae Smith. The story is included in *Hitting Drills and Much More, Poems Short Stories Art* and *Moral Duty*.

Bob had to give up marketing his first two books because he had to raise his children as a single parent. He had to make a choice between his books or children. It wasn't a hard choice; he chose his kids. He published the second edition of *Hitting Drills and Much More* in February 2021. His book, *Moral Duty* is available as an eBook on Amazon, and the soft cover will be available in book stores, as well as Amazon, in 2025. His four children's books, that he co-authored and designed, include, *What is Cool Puppy Doing?, The Book of Bugs, Billy Likes the River*, and *What is Georgie Doing?, and were published* by RIVER MAGIC PUBLISHING, in January 2024: Robert's publishing company.

Bob says, "I have spent the last fifty plus years wondering why I survived the jungles of Vietnam, while my friend and fellow point man, Jack Rae Smith, did not. Over the years I have accepted the responsibilities of raising my three children as a single parent, (see story, "Look Who's Wearing the Apron") had writings published that expressed actions I felt were wrong, and fought for fairness for the disabled, (see story: "Equal Employment for the Disabled"). The dream of writing a book about my experiences while serving in Vietnam have shaped and inspired me to use the "Power of the Pen" to fight against untruths, injustice, discrimination, and inequalities. It all has come down to my moral duty to help advance our world to a better future: all while enjoying the beauty around me and not leave a man behind.

25th Infantry Division Monument

LOOK WHO'S WEARING THE APRON

I was a middle-aged jock in my second year of being Mr. Mom, after changing positions with my ex-wife and taking over primary physical custody of two minor children, while my older daughter stayed with my ex-sister-in-law. No big deal, it was happening more and more often in the nineties when men were accepting the responsibility of caring for their children.

Pencil drawing by twin brother Rich Braun

My story starts on December 15th, 1993 when I moved back into the marital home after over two and a half years of living in a one-bedroom apartment and being an every other weekend Mr. Mom. I had high expectations of molding my kids into highly efficient on-time machines. I was so sure of my persuasive skills that I totally overlooked that I was dealing with a twelve-year old boy and a nine-year old girl. I entered a new life with confidence, believing the household would be running smoothly in a very short time, and was determined to change things by making my home a perfect environment.

Being a morning person who normally got five or six hours of sleep, I saw the everyday responsibilities of washing clothes, doing dishes, and preparing meals as only a slight inconvenience in my everyday routine as a non-mother. I couldn't imagine myself becoming discouraged or sorry about becoming a full-time single parent. There was no way I was going to allow two young children to stop me from reaching my goals.

While growing up in a large family, I watched my mother labor over a scrub board or an old wringer washing machine, washing diaper after diaper for nine children. I was confident that I could manage only two kids in a home with all the modern conveniences of the nineties. I had survived the Army and jungles of Vietnam, so I believed there would be no problem training two out-of-control kids.

It was unbelievable that after only three months I knew what it meant by the saying, being a mother is a thankless job. I abandoned my belief that the kids would be easily molded into self-efficient responsible kids. Instead, was rudely awakened to the fact that any change would take time and a lot more patience than I knew was possible.

I found out what dishpan hands were all about. I also came to understand that for some reason there are always dishes in the sink and that the dryer eats socks; not both socks, but only one of a matching pair. I continued to try, after folding the clothes, to match the single socks with the ever-growing bag of matchless socks and experienced the joy of finding a match. It easily overshadowed the joy of catching a winning touchdown or hitting a game winning grand slam, things I used to think were so important.

I quickly gave up my concept of allowance as a manipulating tool to get my two kids to do their chores, make their lunches and beds, and be nice to each other. Instead, I found myself doing exactly what I used to criticize my ex-wife and mother for doing: just doing things myself instead of battling the kids. It was just easier doing things myself than trying to make them and, damn it, I knew it was wrong.

I don't know why, but I kept hearing myself say things I never accepted before like, "I'm tired of doing everything. You kids better start appreciating what I'm doing for you. You guys better start helping because I can't do it all myself." I think what was happening was the fumes from the dish and laundry detergent were affecting my brain cells, causing me to lose my power. Maybe it was the sudden change in temperature between sticking my head in the refrigerator and standing over the hot stove. Possibly it was the dust of the vacuum cleaner and the lint from folding the clothes. Whatever it was, it was hard to distinguish the difference between being a Mr. Mom, from being a mom. Sometimes, I would go to the bathroom and stand up, just to remember that I was not a member of the so-called, "weaker sex."

I became aware of how little I appreciated a mother's job: the never-ending amount of responsibilities, chores that must be done every day, and making sure everyone else's needs are taken care of before tending to your own; the stress of planning and then cooking meals that would be eaten, making sure everyone had clean clothes to wear, cleaning, and all the other jobs around the house. **It's a job, that's never done!**

I did have a few things going for me, like a great drive to succeed and an appreciation of life; something that I learned in the jungles of Vietnam where I had to fight for my life. Losing my closest friend while serving there also gave me an appreciation of life. Every day I think about my experience in Vietnam and what my mother went through, and use them to inspire me to continue to better myself, work hard, and treasure what I have.

There was no way I was going to abandon my goals of teaching my kids the need to learn and take care of themselves. There was no way I was going to admit failure and give up. Luckily for me, I was already doing some things right.

Each weekend a dish or two was prepared for a quick meal during the week, and there was always homemade spaghetti sauce for a pasta dish. Meals the kids liked were made so they would become confident with my cooking. Fatty foods or sweets were not found in the house, and ready to cook hamburger patties that were mixed from ground turkey and lean hamburger meat were in the freezer.

At least one load of laundry was done almost every night, so it wouldn't become a major job. Most of my social life was doing things with the kids, and free weekends were spent cleaning the house, working in the yard and gardens, and remodeling the home. Probably the smartest thing I did was start talking to women, asking them how they managed their homes and then brought up my problems. Gradually, I began to pick up little bits of information to help me run my household.

Every night I began to pick up to make sure the house was in order before going to bed. I made sure the two kids did the few chores I assigned, was persistent in making sure they maintained proper sleeping habits, and seldom wavered in making sure we all stayed on schedule. Slowly routines were set, habits formed, and both kids started losing weight. My son started to swim without a tee shirt because he was no longer embarrassed about extra weight. I started receiving compliments on how much better the kids looked and behaved.

What helped most was enjoying the little victories, like being able to express my love, tucking them in each night, telling them I loved them, and hearing them respond that they loved me, too. I told my kids that I was only human and made mistakes just like they did. We started to work as a team, and I learned what motivated them.

There were big enjoyments too, like my son excelling in baseball and learning to work hard to improve, my youngest daughter's self-improvements and developing a closer relationship with my older daughter.

My youngest daughter had a learning disability, so she was struggling in school. She was very cold toward me. I spent time with her and made sure she got into a habit of doing her homework as soon as she got home from school. Every night I would check her homework and if it wasn't correct, I would insist that it was done correctly.

Now she did her homework without me telling her, left it out for me to check, and didn't complain when she had to correct a mistake.

Her confidence grew, and she began feeling proud of herself. She did so well that she made the honor roll for the first and second marking periods and got straight A's the third. **I couldn't have been prouder!** My patience and persistence in showing her love melted the ice between us. She became involved in sports and was a happy lovable young lady, always ready for a hug and kiss.

My son had already been a good baseball player; we spent many hours working on it, setting up a weightlifting program for him and hitting off the tee almost every night. By the time the season opened, we were both aware of how much he had improved.

Pencil drawing by
Rich Braun

The baseball team he played on, and I coached, had come in last place the previous two years. The league was the strongest it had been in a long time with no dominating team.

What a year our team had! We went from last to first, winning the playoffs with a record of 17-1. My son hit close to eight hundred and had a pitching record of 12-1.

I went on to manage the 12-year-old All-Star Team. The team won the Southern

12-year-old All-Star Team.

New Jersey State District Championship and came in second and third in two other tournaments. My son was one of the top players, batting third and catching when he wasn't pitching.

Making it through the first year was a major accomplishment. I was now confident in my ability, as a Mr. Mom, to succeed in caring for my children. I was making sure that the house was clean while still maintaining a full and part-time job, coaching both baseball and basketball, writing,

helping the kids in school, and managing all the many other jobs around the house.

Many nights I went to bed tired, but there was always a smile on my face knowing that I'd created a stable, happy, and loving environment for my children. I now know that a mother's job is never done, and appreciate what it takes to be a single parent in the nineties.

Living in Titusville
Washington Crossing

I have lived in the river town of Washington Crossing, New Jersey, for the last sixty-plus years, a place which enabled me to raise my three children as a single parent. It provided a safe place to raise my family and to enjoy the beautiful and historic Delaware River.

Titusville is an unincorporated village about seven miles north of Trenton, the capital of New Jersey. It sits on a high bluff overlooking the beautiful Delaware River and runs between the Delaware Raritan Canal and the river. Four two-lane bridges connect the village to Route 29. A walking and biking trail runs along the canal that was once used by the Belvidere-Delaware Railroad.

Just south of Titusville is Washington Crossing where I live; however, I use the Titusville mailing address. This is where George Washington and his brave men crossed the Delaware River on that cold snowy Christmas night of December 25th, 1776, on America's way to freedom.

The New Jersey Washington Crossing Park is a 3,575-acre park that provides hiking trails, playgrounds, soccer fields, and picnic areas. Many evenings I enjoyed taking my three children to the playgrounds and for walks on the many trails that are cut through the woods of the park. We would

221

sometimes pretend to be American soldiers and any cars would be the British.

The Washington Crossing Bridge connects Titusville and Washington Crossing, New Jersey to Washington Crossing Historic Park in Pennsylvania, that is on the opposite side of the river. The bridge replaced the ferries that ran there during the crossing in 1931.

Both parks are U. S. National Historic Landmarks that were listed on January 30th, 1961 and then placed on it on October 15th, 1966. The picture is from the New Jersey side showing where George Washington and his men crossed from Pennsylvania. Both parks provide a Visitor Center and Museum.

The New Jersey Museum holds the Harry Kels Swan's collection of Revolutionary War artifacts with more than 700 military pieces from both American and British Armies. It also has interpretive exhibits that cover the Revolutionary War to the signing of the Treaty of Paris in 1783.

The New Jersey State Park has an overlook to view the Pennsylvania side where George Washington and his brave men crossed the Delaware and includes three signs explaining the event.

The Reenactment

Every Christmas day since 1953 there is a reenactment of George Washington and his men crossing the Delaware River. Many visitors come from all over the country to visit the parks and watch the reenactment.

During the summers while I was in high school, I worked at the park and learned its history and used the spirit and hardships of those brave men to encourage me to survive the jungles of Vietnam. Over the years, I have water skied, fished, and enjoyed the river; and was always happy to return to Washington Crossing/Titusville, New Jersey, the place I have called home for over sixty-plus year.

Pictures of the reenactment of George Washington
crossing the Delaware River at Washington Crossing
New Jersey and Pennsylvania

These are the three stories that were published in a national magazine in the late 1990s. I had them framed and hung on my wall in my living room.

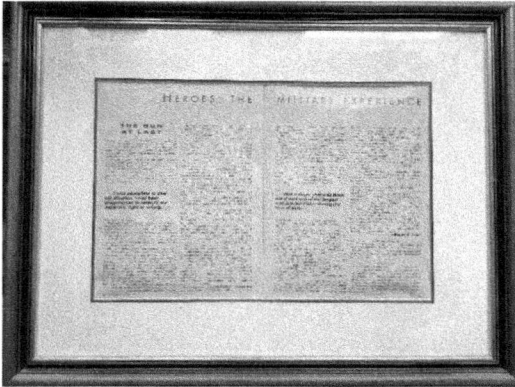

The Sun at Last

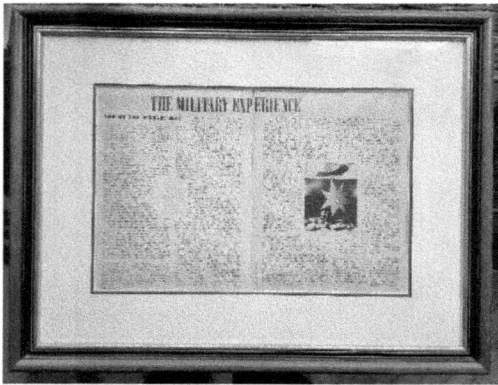

Top of the World Ma!

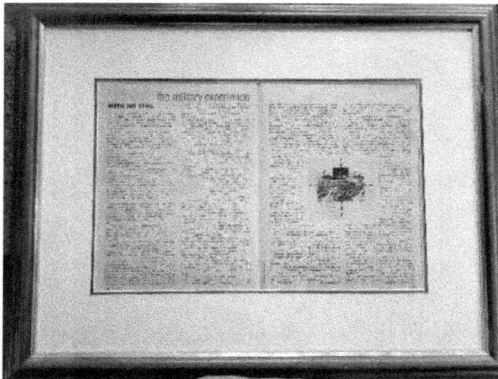

With Me Still

Robert M. Braun, Sr.

Art By Bob
More In Life
I saw and came close to death;
it is why I do more in life.

Using my experiences in Vietnam, the memories of my lost friend Jack, and the inspiration from my twin brother's art, that shows the **beauty of life**, have helped me to look at life with a half full glass. It has motivated me to use the power of the pen and the beauty of the brush to express my appreciation of life on paper and on canvas. Whenever things got tough, I thought, it's not as bad as going to Vietnam and war. I am hoping to set an example to Veterans and others to use their experiences to help us all to a better future and to be positive about life.

The following are examples of some of my art work that I began to develop when I retired from the New Jersey Treasury Department on May 1st 2010. Along with the art, I have put together four books that can be considered a story of my life, along with four childrens' books; one co-authored by my seven-year-old granddaughter, Jenna, one co-authored by my nine-year-old grandson, Andrew, and all four childrens' books, co-authored by Mary L. Maffei.

The four books are: this book "Two Times Dead in Vietnam", "Moral Duty", "Poems Short Stories Art", and "Hitting Drills and Much More". The four children's books include: "What is Cool Puppy Doing?", "The Book of Bugs", "Billy Likes the River", and "What is Georgie Doing?".

Say:
A picture is worth a thousand words.
A pen is worth a million guns.

I wrote this poem many years ago, to help me always to strive to fight untruths, injustice, discrimination, inequalities, and that the use of violence will only lead to more violence. The suffering and misery of war can only be ended

225

by using every means to stop it. It starts with the appreciation of life, the beauty of our world, a Blue Marble in the vastness of space, our home

The following are a few samples of my art that show the **Beauty of Life**.

Acrylic paintings, by Robert M. Braun, Sr.

Reenactment of the Crossing

Blue Heron

A Fall Day

Catch of the Day

*Shopping in the Rain
cover of Poems Short
Stories Art*

Merry Christmas

A Rival

First Snow

The End of the Day

There is the Big One

My Best Friend

Looking for Breakfast

Togetherness

Beautiful Morning

Sunset on My Back Porch

Friendship

Jericho Creek

Pencil Drawings by Robert M. Braun, Sr.

The Holy Family

The Grandkids

A Still Life

A Day at the Beach

References

Ref. 1 https://www.nytimes.com/1983/09/26/obituaries/army-gen-harold-k-johnson-chief-of-staff-from-1964-to-68.html

Ref. 2 https://www.usmarshals.gov/who-we-are/history/historical-reading-room/us-marshals-and-pentagon-riot-of-october-21-1967

Ref. 3 https://www.maderatribune.com/single-post/inside-the-wire-sappers-attack-cu-chi-airfield

Ref. 4 https://www.uso.org/stories/2523-for-40-years-bob-hope-uso-christmas-shows-brightened-the-holidays-for-deployed-troops

Ref. 5 https://www.history.com/topics/vietnam-war/cu-chi-tunnels

Ref. 6 https://www.historynet.com/fire-bases-vietnam/

Ref, 7 https://www.darpa.mil/about-us/timeline/agile-and-m16

Ref. 8 https://www.britannica.com/science/napalm

Ref. 9 https://encyclopedia.pub/entry/28458

Ref. 10 https://man.fas.org/dod-101/sys/land/m60e3.htm

Ref. 11 https://weaponsystems.net/system/792-M79

Ref.12 https://modernfirearms.net/en/assault-rifles/u-s-a-assault-rifles/m14-eng/

Ref. 13 https://achh.army.mil/history/book-vietnam-12evacarjannov70

Ref. 14 https://www.clarioniowa.gov/

Ref. 15 https://www.profootballhof.com/players/franco-harris/

Ref. 16 https://www.visitprinceton.org/things-to-do/historic-sites-and-attractions/princeton-battlefield-state-park/

Ref. 17 https://princetonhistory.org/green-oval-tour/stony-brook-meeting-house.html

Ref. 18 https://www.tpcvc.com/stand-down#:~:text=What%20is%20a%20Stand%20Down,units%20returning%20from%20combat%20operati

Ref. 19 https://www.vietnamonline.com/attraction/ba-den-the-black-virgin-mountain.html

Ref. 20 http://digitaledition.qwinc.com/publication/?i=470668&article_id=2994901&view=articleBrowser

Ref.21 https://www.military.com/equipment/m2-50-caliber-machine-gun

Ref. 22 https://www.boweryboyshistory.com/2010/07/stagecoach-flying-machines-from-new.html

Ref. 23 https://www.fishhabitat.org/waters-to-watch/detail/boone-river-watershed-iowa-retrospective

Ref. 24 https://sofrep.com/specialoperations/claymore-worlds-famous-mine/

Ref. 25 https://www.historyhit.com/the-most-dangerous-viet-cong-booby-traps/

Ref. 26 https://www.thenmusa.org/articles/tunnel-rats-of-the-vietnam-war/

Ref. 27 https://www.navytimes.com/news/your-navy/2019/12/15/arsenal-the-river-patrol-boat-was-the-backbone-of-the-brown-water-navy/

Ref. 28 https://www.military.com/equipment/m72-light-anti-armor-weapon-law

Ref. 29 https://saigoneer.com/saigon-culture/17206-the-harrowing-history-of-vietnam-s-rubber-plantations

Ref. 30 https://www.prc68.com/I/PRS7.html

 Ref. 31 https://www.militaryfactory.com/smallarms/detail.php?smallarms_id=36

Ref. 32 https://cat-uxo.com/explosive-hazards/landmines/md-82b-landmine

Ref. 33 https://vietnamwar.fandom.com/wiki/Landmines_in_the_Vietnam_War

Ref. 34 http://www.vietnamgear.com/kit.aspx?kit=156

Ref.35 https://www.medical-air-service.com/blog/casevac-vs-medevac-the-key-differences_6241.html#:~:text=Casevac%20vs%20Medevac%

Ref.36 https://www.cedars-sinai.org/health-library/tests-and-procedures/c/craniectomy.html#:~:text=A%20craniectomy%20is%20a%20type

Ref. 37 https://en.wikipedia.org › wiki › Long_Bình_Jail

Ref.38 https://cancer.ca/en/cancer-information/cancer-types/neuroblastoma/what-is-neuroblastoma/the-nervous-system#:~:text

Ref. 39 https://www.verywellmind.com/ptsd-from-the-vietnam-war-2797449#:~:text=Incidence%20of%20PTSD%20in%20Vietnam%20Veteran

Ref. 40 https://canalsocietynj.org/canal-history/delaware-and-raritan-canal/#:~:text=The%20canal%20was%20chartered%20in,season%

Ref. 41 https://www.psychologytoday.com/us/blog/twin-dilemmas/202108/insider-s-perspective-how-twins-communicate

Ref. 42 https://www.ninds.nih.gov/health-information/disorders/traumatic-brain-injury-tbi

Ref. 43 https://www.af.mil/About-Us/Biographies/Display/Article/1852720/frank-m-andrews/

Ref. 44 https://walterreed.tricare.mil/About-Us/Facilities/Our-Rich-History#:~:text=Walter%20Reed%20Army%20Medical%20Center,McNair.

Ref. 45 https://www.defense.gov/News/Inside-DOD/Blog/Article/2494459/walter-reed-get-to-know-the-man-behind-the-medical-center/

Ref. 46 https://www.airforcemedicine.af.mil/News/Display/Article/1459865/the-cadillac-of-medevac-the-c9as-lasting-mark-on-the-aeromedic

Ref. 47
https://www.nationalww2museum.org/war/articles/robert-jackson-opening-statement-nuremberg
Ref. 48 Internet Encyclopedia of Philosophy
https://iep.utm.edu › Aristotle-politics

Ref. 49 from the pamphlet "The Crisis", a pamphlet published by the Pennsylvania Journal, during the Revolutionary War 1776.Ref.

50 THE MIRACLE OF AMERICA by William S. Norton, 2010.

Ref. 51 "110 Rules of Civility", George Washington; a set of rules composed by French Jesuits in 1595.

Index

Robert M. Braun, Sr.

Robert M. Braun, Sr.

Jack's Obituary
Military Services
At Church of Christ at 2:30
Friday, April 10th, 1970

Mr. and Mrs. Donald R. Smith of Clarion, Iowa, received word last Thursday of the death of their son, Jack, who was killed in action in Viet Nam, Tuesday, March 31st, 1970.

Military services will be held Friday at 2:30 p. m. at the Church of Christ with the military men from Fort Leavenworth, Kansas. Rev. Owen Wilmoth of Clarion and Rev. Calvin Milan of O'Neill, Nebraska, will officiate.

The flag at the court house and post office was flown at half-mast Thursday afternoon and will be at half-mast until after the services. Those who had flags also displayed them at their homes. Jack is the fifth young man from Wright County to be killed while serving his country.

Jack was born April 18th, 1949 in the Hampton Hospital to Donna and Donald R. Smith of Clarion. Jack graduated from the Clarion High School May 31st, 1967.

He was an all-around athlete. During his high school years, he participated in track, basketball, baseball, and football for four years. His other activities included being class treasurer during his freshman year, and during the sophomore, junior, and senior years he played golf and was a member of the Fellowship of Christian Athletes and of the "C" Club.

He attended Wartburg College in Waverly and made the football team during his freshman year and also earned a letter. His ability in this sport earned him a scholarship at Wartburg.

In the spring of 1969, he entered the armed services, taking his physical examination Wednesday, March 12th, 1969. On Wednesday, June 25th, 1969, he left for the army.

On Friday, October 31st, 1969, he came home from Fort Polk, Louisiana, for a twenty-five-day leave. He left on

Wednesday, November 26th, for Oakland, California.
Thursday, Thanksgiving Day, November 27th, 1969,
he departed for Viet Nam. He was a specialist fourth class.

Wounded in action January 21st he received the Purple Heart. As soon as he recovered he was back with his unit until Tuesday, March 31st, he was killed.

He is survived by his parents, his brother, Ronald, and his brother's wife, Janean, and a niece, Kimberly of Marion: a grandfather, Herman Krueger of Tripoli, and a grandmother, Mrs. Belle Smith of Dows, and many relatives and a host of friends.

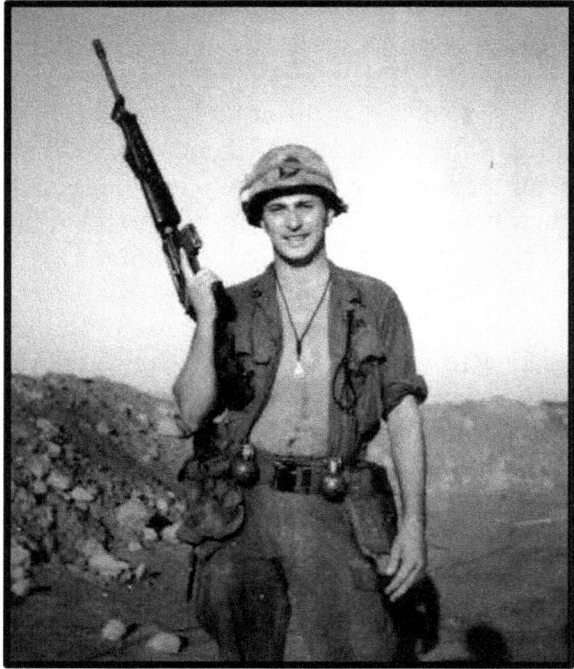

Never forget all those that made
the ultimate sacrifice for our
country and democracy.

Things to Think About:
My biggest concern is the disparity of wealth.

These are things and thoughts that are brought up in my books and what I believe are necessary to give everyone a chance to reach their full potential. As the only intelligent species, is it not our moral duty to advance our world to a better future? These things to think about are at the end of my books : this book "Two Times Dead in Vietnam", "Moral Duty" and "Poems Short Stories Art".

If you average fifty thousand dollars a year, you would have to work twenty thousand years to make a billion dollars. If you made a million dollars a year, you would have to work a thousand years to make a billion dollars. Why does anyone need so much, when so many go without?

It is just like pie, when a small group gets more of the pie, everyone else gets less.

In 1945 the highest tax rate was 94% on anything over $200,000. There were 27 steps in the progressive income tax. This enabled our country to get through the Great Depression and WWII with a small amount of debt. In 2024 the highest income tax rate is 37% and there are only 7 steps. This is why we have such a large national debt today. We are not taxing those that have the most, at a higher rate.

A recent report tells us that there are 2,781 billionaires in the world today. Their combined wealth, if they were a country, would be the third wealthiest in the world, after the United States and China. Again, why is it right that so few have so much?

Robert M. Braun, Sr.

Why, is there such a low cap on the amount of income you pay into Social Security? In 2024 the cap is $168,600. In other words, you pay no more than $10,453, no matter how much you make. So, it is a low-income tax. Increase the cap and you'll save Social Security and the seniors could receive more.

With today's technology a small group or an individual could control the entire world. It has happened throughout history, where a small group controlled everything: The Pharaohs of Egypt, the rulers of The Roman Empire, the Kings of Europe. It is now possible to control the entire world and the process of it is happening now.

We all come into this world with equal rights to the riches of our world. Why is it right that some have so much while others have so little? Is it because, as Benjamin Franklin found out in 1758, "Those who have the money make the rules"?

For Further Reading

CLARION STORIES
A LOVE LETTER TO IOWA
By Dennis E. Hoffman

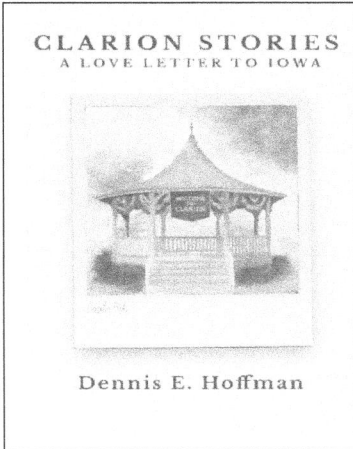

ISBN: 979-8-9938645-0-1
USA $15.99

Art on the cover done by:
Erin Hoffman

Dennis E. Hoffman returns to his roots inspired by his Alzheimer's stricken mother, Loree. Hoffman crafts a luminous collection of heartfelt stories about ordinary people doing extraordinary things.

Some of the stories included are: "Just the Town Historians", "The Cocooning of Jim Cook", "Dad's Kept Promise", "When Pride Still Mattered", "Racism Rears Its Ugly Head", "A Picture of Inspiration", "Friends Forever", "Echo of a Train Whistle", "Keys to Success", "Color Blind Clarion", "Trail Blazer", "Be True to Yourself", "Vietnam War Lays Waste to Hometown Hero", "Die Hard", "Happy Trails".

The book Clarion Stories along with other books written by Dennis E Hoffman are available at Amazon.

Life
Life came from nothing
to fill the emptiness of space
so that
The Heavens could live.

The End
I hope you
enjoyed the book.

www.ingramcontent.com/pod-product-compliance
Lightning Source LLC
Chambersburg PA
CBHW060018100426
42740CB00010B/1516